NOLO'S LAW FORM KIT

Leases & Rental Agreements

By David Brown & Ralph Warner

Edited by Lisa Goldoftas & Marcia Stewart

NOLO PRESS   BERKELEY

YOUR RESPONSIBILITY WHEN USING A SELF-HELP LAW KIT

We've done our best to give you useful and accurate information in this kit. But this kit does not take the place of a lawyer licensed to practice law in your state. If you want legal advice, see a lawyer. If you use any information contained in this kit, it's your personal responsibility to make sure that the facts and general information contained in it are applicable to your situation.

KEEPING UP-TO-DATE

To keep its kits up-to-date, Nolo Press issues new printings and new editions periodically. New printings reflect minor legal changes and technical corrections. New editions contain major legal changes, major text additions or major reorganizations. To find out if a later printing or edition of any Nolo kit is available, call Nolo Press at (510) 549-1976 or check the catalog in the *Nolo News,* our quarterly newspaper.

To stay current, follow the "Update" service in the *Nolo News.* You can get the paper free by sending us the registration card in this kit. In another effort to help you use Nolo's latest materials, we offer a 25% discount off the purchase of any new Nolo kit or book if you turn in any earlier printing or edition. (See the "Recycle Offer" in the back of this booklet.)

FIRST EDITION	January 1994
BOOK DESIGN	Terri Hearsh
COVER DESIGN	Brad Thomas
PRODUCTION	Stephanie Harolde
	Dave McFarland

ISBN 0-87337-228-X

Copyright © 1994 by Nolo Press

All Rights Reserved

TABLE OF CONTENTS

How To Use This Kit 3

When You Need Help Beyond This Kit 3

Leases and Rental Agreements—An Overview 5

Before You Fill In a Lease or Rental Agreement Form 6

Fill In a Draft Lease or Rental Agreement Form 7
    Clause 1. Identification of Landlord and Tenants 8
    Clause 2. Identification of Premises and Occupants 8
    Clause 3. Limits on Use and Occupancy 9
    Clause 4. Defining the Term of the Tenancy 9
    Clause 5. Amount and Schedule for the Payment of Rent 9
    Clause 6. Late Charges 12
    Clause 7. Returned Check and Other Bank Charges 12
    Clause 8. Amount and Payment of Deposits 12
    Clause 9. Utilities 16
    Clause 10. Prohibition of Assignment and Subletting 16
    Clause 11. Condition of the Premises 16
    Clause 12. Possession of the Premises 18
    Clause 13. Pets 18
    Clause 14. Landlord's Access for Inspection and Emergency 18
    Clause 15. Extended Absences By Tenants 18
    Clause 16. Prohibitions Against Violating Laws and Causing Disturbances 20
    Clause 17. Repairs and Alterations 20
    Clause 18. Damage to Premises 20
    Clause 19. Tenants' Financial Responsibility and Renters' Insurance 21
    Clause 20. Waterbeds 21
    Clause 21. Tenant Rules and Regulations 21
    Clause 22. Payment of Attorney Fees in a Lawsuit 21
    Clause 23. Authority to Receive Legal Papers 22
    Clause 24. Additional Provisions 22
    Clause 25. Entire Agreement 22

Finding Suitable Tenants 24

Prepare, Sign and Distribute the Lease or Rental Agreement 29

Get the Tenants Moved In 31

Appendix 1: Rent Control Chart 33

Appendix 2: Lease & Rental Agreement Forms 45

HOW TO USE THIS KIT

This form kit helps you prepare your own valid California lease or rental agreement. The fill-in-the-blanks forms in this kit can be customized to fit your situation. Simply follow the step-by-step instructions in this kit and use common sense. There is normally no need to hire a lawyer.

To best use this kit, follow these steps:

Step 1. Read the overview (page 5).

Step 2. Select the lease or rental agreement form you need.

Step 3. Carefully follow the step-by-step instructions and prepare a rough draft of the lease or rental agreement.

Step 4. After you've found suitable tenants, neatly type or print their names and other needed information onto a final version of your lease or rental agreement.

Step 5. Collect your tenants' security deposit and first month's rent.

Step 6. You and each tenant sign and date the lease or rental agreement.

Step 7. Make a photocopy of the signed form and provide the tenants with a copy, keeping the original for your own records.

Step 8. Get your tenants moved in.

LOOK FOR THESE ABBREVIATIONS AND ICONS

CC refers to the California Civil Code, a set of state laws that define many of California landlords' rights and responsibilities.

CCP refers to the California Code of Civil Procedure, a set of state laws that include procedural aspects of California landlord/tenant laws.

 A caution to slow down and consider potential problems.

 "Fast track" lets you know that you may be able to skip some material that doesn't apply to your situation.

Applies only to cities with rent control ordinances—Berkeley, Beverly Hills, Campbell (mediation only), Cotati, East Palo Alto, Hayward, Los Angeles, Los Gatos, Oakland, Palm Springs, San Francisco, San Jose, Santa Monica, Thousand Oaks and West Hollywood.

WHEN YOU NEED HELP BEYOND THIS KIT

Preparing a lease or rental agreement with this kit is ordinarily simple and straightforward. In some circumstances, however, you may need additional information. *The Landlord's Law Book*, a two-volume set published by Nolo Press, can help with your questions:

- *Volume 1, Rights and Responsibilities*, by attorneys David Brown and Ralph Warner, concentrates on the legal rules associated with most aspects of renting and managing residential real property in California. In addition to information on leases and rental agreements, it covers essential legal and practical information regarding security deposits, rent control laws and anti-discrimination laws, as well as tenants' right to privacy and the landlord's duty to maintain the premises in a habitable condition. In addition, this essential landlord's guide shows you how to raise rent and change other terms of the tenancy, how to legally terminate tenancies, and how to hire and work with managers. It also explains how to find and use statutes and, if necessary, how to find and work with a lawyer. The book contains practical, easy-to-use checklists and sample forms.

- *Volume 2, Evictions*, by attorney David Brown, contains all the forms and instructions necessary to end a tenancy, including a step-by-step guide to handling your own eviction proceeding in court.

(For information on ordering books from Nolo Press, see the back of this kit.)

WHAT THIS KIT DOESN'T COVER

This kit doesn't cover...	Explanation	Where to get help
commercial leases and rental agreements	Commercial and business leases typically contain complex clauses that a lawyer should draft.	Consider seeing a lawyer.
how to hire a resident property manager to handle day-to-day management of your rental property	By hiring a property manger, you enter into an employer-employee relationship. Legal obligations that arise from such an arrangement are beyond the scope of this kit.	You may want to use a property management firm to handle all employment-related matters. Or see *The Landlord's Law Book, Volume 1: Rights and Responsibilities*, by David Brown & Ralph Warner (Nolo Press).
Spanish-language leases and rental agreements	If your lease or written month-to-month rental agreement is negotiated primarily in Spanish, you must give the tenant notice in Spanish of her right to request a Spanish translation of the lease or rental agreement. (CC § 1632.) We recommend that you routinely make Spanish-language translations available to tenants who speak Spanish as their first language.	To get copies of a Spanish-language lease, contact the California Apartment Association, 1414 K St., Suite 610, Sacramento, CA 95814, 916-447-7881.
very short-term rentals (such as daily or weekly) or rentals of mobile homes, condominiums, boarding houses or hotels	The information in this kit covers the laws geared toward long-term residential leases and rental agreements.	Consider seeing a lawyer.
leases and rental agreements for low-income tenants who have signed up for a federally subsidized housing assistance program	The most common federally subsidized housing assistance is the Section 8 program of the federal Department of Housing and Urban Development (HUD). "Section 8" refers to Section 8 of the United States Housing Act of 1937, 42 USC 1437f. That program subsidizes tenants' rents by paying part of the rent directly to the landlord. Lease formats are dictated by governmental regulations and are drafted by HUD or a local "Housing Authority." You cannot insist on drafting your own lease. You have the right to refuse to rent on a Section 8 basis without violating any anti-discrimination laws.	Call the housing authority in the county where your property is located if you wish to participate in the Section 8 program. They will refer eligible applicants to you and will prepare the necessary documents, including the lease, as well as a one-year agreement between you and the housing authority.

LEASES AND RENTAL AGREEMENTS—AN OVERVIEW

To prepare your own lease or rental agreement correctly, you'll need to understand some key legal concepts and terminology. Here are the basics.

What Are Leases and Rental Agreements?

There are two kinds of written landlord/tenant arrangements:

- rental agreements, and
- leases.

Written **rental agreements** provide for a tenancy for an indefinite period of time, and can be terminated by either party by the giving of a written notice, very commonly 30 days. Where the rent is paid monthly, these are called "month-to-month" tenancies. They automatically renew each month (or other time period agreed to in writing) unless one of the parties gives the other the proper amount of written notice (30 days for a month-to-month tenancy, unless rent control laws provide otherwise) and terminates the agreement. The rental agreements in this kit are month-to-month.

With a written **lease**, you fix the term of the tenancy—most often for six months or a year, but sometimes longer. At the end of the lease term, you have a few options. You can:

- decline to renew the lease
- sign a new lease for a set period, or
- do nothing—which means your lease will revert to a month-to-month tenancy if you continue to accept monthly rent from the tenant.

The people involved in the lease or rental agreement—the landlord and the tenant—are referred to in legal jargon as **parties**. Any competent adult—at least 18 years of age—may be a party to a lease or rental agreement. (A teenager under age 18 may also be a party to a lease if he or she has achieved legal adult status through a court order, military service or marriage.)

WHY YOU SHOULD "GET IT IN WRITING"

Oral (spoken) leases or rental agreements are legal for month-to-month tenancies, and for leases for a year or less. (CC § 1624.) But it is never wise to rely on an oral agreement. As time passes and circumstances change, people's memories—including yours—have a funny habit of becoming unreliable.

From the landlord's point of view, failure to prepare a written agreement invites trouble. You can almost count on tenants claiming that certain oral promises weren't kept or "forgetting" key agreements.

Most landlords choose to impose conditions on the tenancy, such as regulating or prohibiting pets and subletting. In addition, landlords often include a clause providing the landlord with the right to recover attorney fees if it is necessary to evict a tenant.

Oral leases, while legal, are even more dangerous than oral rental agreements because they require that one important term—the length of the lease—be accurately remembered by both parties over a considerable time. If something goes wrong with an oral agreement, the parties are all too likely to end up in court, arguing over who said what to whom, when and in what context.

Leases, Rental Agreements and the Law

Under California law, landlords must follow legal rules when renting residential property. All key rules are covered in instructions for the forms in this kit.

As a landlord, it's important to understand that it is illegal to circumvent the law—even if it's okay with the tenant. If you violate the law, the tenant can sue you. In addition, you could face a lawsuit and fines by the district attorney.

Example 1: Natalie wants to rent out a small house located in Santa Monica. The local rent control ordinance sets the rent for this particular house at $650. Because the house is in a prime location, Jerome is eager to be selected as the tenant. He offers to pay Natalie $850 rent, which is $200 more than she is entitled to receive. By law, Natalie cannot rent her property under this arrangement. If she does, Jerome may later sue for up to three times the excess rent, plus attorney fees and costs. (CC § 1947.11.) Natalie also could face charges by the district attorney for violating local rent control ordinances.

Example 2: Yasser has a policy of refusing to rent to tenants with pets. He refuses to rent to Ariel, who is legally blind, because she has a seeing-eye dog. This is illegal, and Yasser could face a civil suit, even though he honestly didn't know he was violating a state civil rights law.

BEFORE YOU FILL IN A LEASE OR RENTAL AGREEMENT FORM

Before you prepare your lease or rental agreement form, you need to take these two steps:

Step 1. Choose between a fixed-term lease and a month-to-month rental agreement.

Step 2. Check to see if your property is covered by local rent control ordinances. If so, you'll need to comply with those laws.

Step 1: Choose Between a Lease and a Rental Agreement

There isn't much legal difference between a lease and a rental agreement—with the exception, of course, of the period of occupancy. To decide whether a lease or rental agreement is better for you, read what follows and carefully think about your own situation.

Month-to-Month Rental Agreement

When you rent property under a month-to-month rental agreement, these rules apply:

- **On 30 days' written notice, you may change the amount of rent (subject to any rent control ordinances).** You may increase (or decrease) the amount of rent in all areas that don't have rent control ordinances. Cities with rent control ordinances may restrict the amount of rent you may charge or add requirements for notifying the tenant of a rent increase.

- **On 30 days' written notice, you may change other terms of the tenancy.** You may make other changes in the terms of the tenancy, such as increasing the deposit amount, adding or modifying a no-pets clause or making any other reasonable change. Again, however, cities with rent control ordinances may restrict your right to do this.

- **You may end the tenancy with 30 days' written notice.** Except in certain rent control cities, you may end the tenancy at any time, as long as you give 30 days' advance warning. Not surprisingly, many landlords prefer to rent from month-to-month, particularly in urban areas where new tenants can often be found in a few days.

- **A tenant who wants to leave needs to give you only 30 days' notice.** From a landlord's point of view, a month-to-month tenancy can mean more tenant turnover. Tenants who know they may legally move out with only 30 days' notice may be more inclined to do so than tenants who make a longer commitment. If you live in an area where it's difficult to find tenants, you may wisely want tenants to commit for a longer time period, such as a year.

Fixed-Term Lease

With a fixed-term lease, these rules apply:

- **You can't raise the rent until the lease runs out.** The only exception applies where the lease says you may raise the rent, and local rent control laws don't limit rent increases.

- **You can't change other terms of the tenancy.** A lease is a contract whose terms are fixed for the lease period. Changes are allowed only where the lease says they're allowed, or where the tenant agrees in writing to a modification of the terms.

- **You usually can't evict before the lease term expires.** Unless the tenant fails to pay the rent or violates another significant term of the lease, such as repeatedly making too much noise or damaging the property, you're stuck with the tenant until the lease term runs out.

- **You may reduce your turnover rate.** Many people make a serious personal commitment when they enter into a long-term lease, in part because they think they'll be liable for quite a few months' rent if they up and leave. So, leases are usually preferable in areas where there is a high vacancy rate or it is difficult to find tenants.

> **Reality check:** A savvy tenant can often get out of a lease, with little or no financial risk, although a lease may increase the likelihood of keeping tenants for longer periods. By law, if a tenant leaves before the lease term expires, you have an obligation to try to rent the unit to another suitable tenant at the same or a greater rent. Only if you can't find another suitable tenant to move in would the tenant who leaves be liable for the unpaid rent. Knowing this, many tenants who wish to break a lease produce a new tenant to take over. Even if you don't want to rent to this person, chances are it won't be productive to try and recover money from the lease-breaking tenant.

Step 2: Check Any Rent Control Ordinances

> **If your property isn't governed by rent control:** Skip the rest of this section and go on to "Fill In a Draft Lease or Rental Agreement Form," below, unless your rental property is located in a city with some type of rent control. These cities are: Berkeley, Beverly Hills, Campbell (mediation only), Cotati, East Palo Alto, Hayward, Los Angeles, Los Gatos,

Oakland, Palm Springs, San Francisco, San Jose, Santa Monica, Thousand Oaks and West Hollywood.

No two rent control ordinances are identical, so it's important that you become familiar with your city's rent control laws. For example:

- Some cities have elected or appointed rent control boards that have the power to adjust rents across the board. Others automatically allow a certain percentage rent increase each year as part of their ordinances. All cities provide that the elected or appointed board, or a hearing officer, may allow an increase (or decrease) in rents, on a case-by-case basis.

- Many cities' ordinances govern how—and under what circumstances—a landlord may terminate a tenancy, even one from month-to-month, by requiring the landlord to have just cause (a valid reason) to evict. These reasons are set out in the city ordinance, and typically include such things as the tenant violating the lease or rental agreement (including not paying rent), the tenant committing an illegal activity, or the landlord wanting to move himself or a family member into the property.

- Some cities require landlords to register their properties with a local rent control agency.

- Some rent control ordinances have a feature called "vacancy decontrol" that allows landlords free rein to raise the rent when a unit is vacated.

- Several cities require the landlord to pay interest on the tenant's security deposits. Some cities impose notice requirements for rent increases and termination of tenancies that are different from the state law requirements.

Get Up-to-Date Information

If your rental property is in a city with rent control, it is imperative that you contact the city's rent control board for an up-to-date copy of the local ordinance and any regulations interpreting it. Check the Rent Control Chart in Appendix 1 for the address of your local rent control board.

In addition, your local apartment owners' association can give you general information on rent control ordinances in your area. For the name of your local association, contact the California Apartment Association, 1414 K St., Suite 610, Sacramento, CA 95814, 916-447-7881.

PROPERTY EXEMPT FROM RENT CONTROL

Not all rental housing within a rent-controlled city is subject to rent control. Units in buildings constructed in the last decade, as well as owner-occupied buildings with four (or sometimes three or two) units or less, are often exempt from rent control ordinances. Some cities also exempt single-family dwellings and luxury units that rent for more than a certain amount.

Unfortunately, an ordinance can sometimes be ambiguous, leaving the landlord and tenant to wonder whether or not the property is covered. If the local rent board can't give you a straight answer—or you're reluctant to contact them—you may need to consult an attorney who's familiar with your community's rent control ordinance. Check the Yellow Pages for attorneys who specialize in "landlord/tenant" law, and whose offices are in the city where your rental property is located.

FILL IN A DRAFT LEASE OR RENTAL AGREEMENT FORM

We strongly urge you to take the time to prepare a rough draft of a lease or rental agreement *before* you look for suitable tenants. By doing this, you will educate yourself about the laws affecting your rental property and be able to make educated decisions about the terms of the tenancy. If, for example, prospective tenants claim they have the right to keep a pet because the next door neighbor has two dogs, you'll know that simply isn't the law.

GUIDELINES FOR CREATING A ROUGH DRAFT

Here are some suggestions for completing your rough draft.

Read the instructions carefully. The instructions for each clause not only tell you what to put in the blanks, but provide the background necessary to comply with the law.

Photocopy the blank forms. Two blank copies of the lease and rental agreement forms are provided in Appendix 2 of this kit. Photocopy the forms before you use the last blank copy. That way, you'll have an extra copy in case you make a mistake or need to use the forms again.

Clearly mark changes. If you change any clauses, make clear notes so you won't miss putting them onto your final draft.

Add pages if necessary. If you want to make a lengthy addition to the lease or rental agreement, you can write or type it on a separate sheet of paper and attach it to the final form. (Instructions for preparing Attachment pages are covered in "How To Prepare Attachment Pages," page 29.)

The Fixed-Term Residential Lease and Month-to-Month Residential Rental Agreement forms in this kit are identical, with the exception of Clause 4: Defining the Terms of the Tenancy.

Here's how to fill in the form you've selected. (Guidelines on choosing between the forms are covered in "Step 1: Choose Between a Lease and a Rental Agreement," page 6.)

Clause 1. Identification of Landlord and Tenants

You'll need to specify who will be responsible for renting your property. Leave this blank for now; you'll fill it in after you've found suitable tenants.

When you've settled on tenants and are ready to prepare a final lease, fill in the date you'll be signing. Next, fill in the names of *all* adults who will live in the premises. If anyone else will be financially responsible for paying the rent (even if they won't be living in the premises), list their names.

In the last blank, list the names of all landlords.

The last sentence states that the tenants are both jointly and severally liable for paying rent and adhering to the terms of the agreement. This means that each tenant is responsible for the whole agreement and rent, as well as his or her portion of the rent. This protects the landlord, who can legally seek full compensation from any or all of the tenants should a problem arise.

Clause 2. Identification of Premises and Occupants

In this clause, you identify the property being rented and who will live in it. The words "for residential purposes only" are to prevent a tenant from using the property for conducting a business—for example, a day-care center that might affect your insurance or violate zoning laws.

> ⚠ **If tenants want to run a business on the premises:** Before agreeing to let a tenant conduct any sort of business on the property, check on zoning laws and consult your insurance company as to whether you'll need a more expensive policy to cover potential liability of employees or guests. You may also wish to explore the possibility of requiring the tenant to maintain certain types of insurance coverage, so that you won't wind up paying if something goes awry.

In the first blank, fill in the address of the unit or house. If there is an apartment number, specify that as well. Include the city where the property is located.

In shared housing situations, you'll need to clearly state, in your own words, what the rental includes.

> **Example:** You are renting a small cottage in your backyard that comes with kitchen privileges in your house. You might fill in, "Back cottage at 1212 Parker St., Visalia, California, with kitchen privileges in main house."

If you need more room, perhaps to explain what the kitchen privileges or other rental conditions include, start by filling in the address of the property. Then add the words "as more fully described in Attachment 1 to this Agreement." Next, prepare a separate "Attachment 1" and define the particulars of what you are renting. (Guidelines on preparing attachments are covered in "How To Prepare Attachment Pages," page 29.)

If any particular part of the property is not being rented, such as a garage or shed you wish to use yourself or rent to someone else, make this clear by specifically excluding it from your description of the premises. If you don't, the tenant has rented it.

> **Example:** "Single-family house at 1210 Parker St., Visalia, California, except for the two-car garage."

In the last blank, list the names of any minor children who will be living in the rental property, or put "None," as appropriate. If, however, you are worried about the possibility of overcrowding if the family has more children, you should state the number of minor children—"Two children, Adam and Amy." (Don't discriminate against children; see "How Many Occupants To Allow," below.)

HOW MANY OCCUPANTS TO ALLOW

You can legally establish reasonable space-to-people ratios, but you cannot use overcrowding as a euphemism for refusing to rent to tenants with children. Discrimination against families with children is illegal, except in housing reserved for senior citizens only.

To avoid discriminating against families with children, your safest bet is to adopt an across-the-board "two-plus-one" policy: you allow two persons per bedroom plus one additional occupant. Thus, a landlord who draws the line at three people to a one-bedroom, five to a two-bedroom, and seven to a three-bedroom unit will be on a safe ground in this regard. However, a landlord is asking for trouble by insisting on two or fewer people in a one-bedroom unit, four or fewer in a two-bedroom unit and so on, unless you have a legitimate reason for the restrictive standards.

Most important, maintain a consistent occupancy policy. If you allow three adults to live in a two-bedroom apartment, you had better let a couple with a child live in the same type of unit, or you leave yourself open to charges that you are illegally discriminating.

Finally, do not inquire as to the age and sex of any two children who will be sharing a bedroom. This is their parents' business, not yours.

(For a much more in-depth discussion of the area of discrimination, see *The Landlord's Law Book, Volume 1: Rights and Responsibilities,* by attorneys David Brown and Ralph Warner (Nolo Press), Chapter 9.)

Clause 3. Limits on Use and Occupancy

This clause lets the tenants know they may not move anyone else in as a permanent resident without your consent.

When it comes to restricting how long guests may stay, it usually makes sense to include a reasonable time limit in your lease or rental agreement. Even if you do not want to enforce restrictions on guests strictly, this provision will be very handy to have if a tenant tries to move in a friend or relative for a month or two, calling her a guest. It will give you leverage to either ask the guest to leave or to request that the guest become a tenant with an appropriate increase in rent. Restrictions on guests may not be based on the age or sex of the occupant or guest.

You don't need to add anything to this clause.

Clause 4. Defining the Term of the Tenancy

If you're using the Fixed-Term Residential Lease form, follow the instructions for "Fixed-Term Lease Provision," just below, then skip to Clause 5. If you're using the Month-to-Month Residential Rental Agreement, follow the "Month-to-Month Rental Agreement Provision" instructions below.

Fixed-Term Lease Provision

The lease form provision sets a definite date for the beginning and expiration of the lease. It also includes a warning that explains the tenants' liability for breaking the lease.

In the blanks, fill in the starting date and the expiration date. Leases usually last six, 12 or 24 months, but of course, this is up to you and the tenants.

Month-to-Month Rental Agreement Provision

In the blank, fill in the date the tenancy will begin. With this clause, you'll need to give tenants 30 days' written notice before changing or terminating their tenancy. While this is the most common notice period, other options are available; you can simply cross out "30 days" and write in another time frame. Here are your options:

- **more than 30 days' notice.** You may want to agree that the tenants get a longer notice period—say 60 or 90 days. Some landlords report that they file fewer eviction lawsuits when they give tenants a generous amount of time in which to find another place.
- **less than 30 days' notice.** The law allows a rental agreement to contain a clause giving as little as seven days' notice to terminate a tenancy. (CC § 1946.) Though this may at first seem advantageous to landlords, it's not usually a good idea because the tenant could terminate the tenancy on short notice, too. In addition, it's questionable whether you can use this sort of short-notice clause to terminate a tenancy in less than 30 days if you have already accepted rent to cover a period beyond the end of the short-notice period. In other words, if you accept rent on January 1 for the whole month, your seven-day notice may not be valid unless served on or after the 24th, to take effect on the first day not covered by rent you've already accepted.

A landlord's right to terminate or change the terms of a tenancy, even one from month-to-month, is limited by local rent control ordinances. Such ordinances not only limit rent and other terms of tenancies, but also require the landlord to have a good reason to terminate a tenancy. (We discuss rent control in "Step 2: Check Any Rent Control Ordinances," on page 6.)

Clause 5. Amount and Schedule for the Payment of Rent

Before you fill in the blanks, read the following discussion about rental charges and payments.

How Much Can You Charge?

No state or federal laws govern how much rent landlords can charge. Unless your premises are subject to a local rent control ordinance, you can legally charge as much rent as you want (or more practically speaking, as much as a tenant will pay).

If you're renting in a rent control city, follow the rules for setting a legal amount of rent. (Rent control is discussed on page 6 and detailed summaries are provided in Appendix 1.)

If you are new to the rental business, you may wish to check newspaper want-ads for comparable rents in your area, or contact local real estate and property management companies. Some landlords choose to charge slightly less than the going rate as part of a policy designed to find and keep excellent tenants.

When Rent Is Due

Most lease and rental agreements, including the ones in this kit, call for rent to be paid monthly, in advance. The first day of the month is customary, but it is perfectly legal to require rent to be paid on a different day of the month. This may make sense if the tenant is paid at odd times or the tenant moves in in the middle of the month. However, in this latter situation, many landlords find it easiest to pro-rate rent for a short first month and then require that rent be paid on the first of the next month. (That option is covered in Clause 5b, below.)

Also, you should understand that you are not legally required to have your tenant pay rent on a monthly basis. If you wish, you and the tenant can agree that the rent be paid twice a month, each week, or on whatever schedule suits you. You could simply modify the clause; if so, clearly set out the arrangement. For example: "Tenants shall pay to Landlord a monthly rent of $800, payable in advance in installments of $400 on the first and 15th of the month."

> ⚠ **Month-to-month rental agreement notice:** If you use a rental agreement, you should be aware that the notice period you must give your tenant to terminate or change the terms of the tenancy (and the notice the tenant must give you) is normally the same number of days as the period between rent payments—typically 30 days. (CC § 827.) This is true unless your rental agreement specifically establishes a different notice period, or a local rent control ordinance rules otherwise.

As indicated in the agreement, when rent would actually be due on a Saturday, Sunday or holiday, it is legally due on the next business day.

> **Example:** If your lease or rental agreement says a tenant's rent is due on the first day of each month, and April 1 falls on Saturday, rent isn't due until Monday, April 3. If April 3 is a legal holiday, rent isn't legally due until Tuesday, April 4.

LATE RENT: THERE IS NO SUCH THING AS AN AUTOMATIC GRACE PERIOD

Now let's clear up a giant myth. Lots of tenants are absolutely convinced that if they pay by the 5th (or sometimes the 7th or even the 10th) of the month, they have legally paid their rent on time and should suffer no penalty because they are within a legal grace period. Not true. There is no law that automatically gives tenants a grace period when it comes to paying the rent. It's up to you to decide whether or not you want a grace period. It's also up to you to enforce any penalties for paying rent late, such as a late charge or even eviction proceedings.

In practice, some tenants get a grace period because their landlord doesn't get upset unless rent is more than a few days late. But you are definitely within your legal rights to insist that the rent be paid on the day it is due, or a day or two later, allowing for Saturdays, Sundays and legal holidays.

Where and How Rent Is To Be Paid

It is not necessary to specify in your lease or rental agreement where, or even how, the tenant should pay her rent. Assuming you don't, normal business practice generally controls how rent is paid until you properly notify the tenant in writing of a change. For example, a tenant can reasonably assume it's okay to send the rent by mail. However, it is perfectly legal to designate where and how the rent is paid. You might, for example, require that rent be paid personally, at your place of business. This makes the tenant responsible for getting the rent to you at a certain time or place, and avoids issues such as whether or not the rent was lost or delayed in the mail.

You may wish to specify whether rent should be paid by cash, check or money order. Some landlords, concerned with security and the need to write receipts, accept checks only. Others are more concerned about bounced checks and will accept only cash, certified checks or money orders.

Fill In Clause 5

Specify the amount of monthly rent in the first blank. Then indicate when the monthly rent is to be paid—usually on the first of the month. Next, specify to whom and where the rent is to be paid.

5a. If you want to specify what form of payment you'll accept—such as cash, cashier's check, personal check or money order—check the box and fill in the blank.

5b. If the Tenants move in before the regular rental period—let's say on June 19, and you want rent due on the first of every month—you can specify the pro-rated amount due for the first month. That will avoid any question or confusion about what you expect to be paid. Specify the move-in date and the ending date of that rental period, such as "June 19, 1995 through June 30, 1995." Divide the monthly rent by 30 (even for 31-day months or February—it's easier) and multiply by the number of days in the first rental period. For example, $900/30 = $30. $30 x 12 days = $360. Finally, fill in the pro-rated amount due.

FIXED-TERM RESIDENTIAL LEASE

1. **Identification of Landlord and Tenants.** This Agreement is made and entered into on _November 14_, 19_9X_, between _Sharon and Hank Donaldson_ ("Tenants") and _Lionel Jones_ ("Landlord"). Each Tenant is jointly and severally liable for the payment of rent and performance of all other terms of this Agreement.

2. **Identification of Premises and Occupants.** Subject to the terms and conditions set forth in this Agreement, Landlord rents to Tenants, and Tenants rent from Landlord, for residential purposes only, the premises located at _123 Sendaro Street, Fresno_, California ("the premises"). The premises shall be occupied by the undersigned Tenants and the following minor children: _Jan Donaldson_.

3. **Limits on Use and Occupancy.** The premises are to be used only as a private residence for Tenants and any minors listed in Clause 2 of this Agreement, and for no other purpose without Landlord's prior written consent. Occupancy by guests for more than ten days in any six-month period is prohibited without Landlord's written consent and shall be considered a breach of this Agreement.

4. **Defining the Term of the Tenancy.** The term of the rental shall begin on _December 1_, 19_9X_, and shall expire on _November 30_, 19_9X_. Should Tenants vacate before expiration of the term, Tenants shall be liable for the balance of the rent for the remainder of the term, less any rent Landlord collects or could have collected from a replacement tenant by reasonably attempting to re-rent. Tenants who vacate before expiration of the term are also responsible for Landlord's costs of advertising for a replacement tenant.

5. **Amount and Schedule for the Payment of Rent.** Tenants shall pay to Landlord a monthly rent of $ _775.00_, payable in advance on the _1st_ day of each month, except when that day falls on a weekend or legal holiday, in which case rent is due on the next business day. Rent shall be paid to _Lionel Jones_ at _125 Sendaro Street, Fresno, California 93656_, or at such other place as Landlord shall designate from time to time.

    ☒ a. The form of payment shall be _check_.

    ☐ b. On signing this Agreement, Tenants shall pay to Landlord for the period of _____, 19___, through _____, 19___, the sum of $_____ as rent, payable in advance.

6. **Late Charges.** Tenants shall pay Landlord a late charge if Tenants fail to pay the rent in full within _five_ days after the date it is due. The late charge shall be $_5.00_, plus $_5.00_ for each additional day that the rent continues to be unpaid. The total late charge for any one month shall not exceed $_35.00_. Landlord does not waive the right to insist on payment of the rent in full on the date it is due.

7. **Returned Check and Other Bank Charges.** In the event any check offered by Tenants to Landlord in payment of rent or any other amount due under this Agreement is returned for lack of sufficient funds, a "stop payment" or any other reason, Tenants shall pay Landlord a returned check charge in the amount of $_20.00_.

8. **Amount and Payment of Deposits.** On signing this Agreement, Tenants shall pay to Landlord the sum of $_1,000.00_ as a security deposit. Tenants may not, without Landlord's prior written consent, apply this security deposit to the last month's rent or to any other sum due under this Agreement. Within three weeks after Tenants have vacated the premises, Landlord shall furnish Tenants with an itemized written statement of the reasons for, and the dollar amount of, any of the security deposit retained by the Landlord, along with a check for any deposit balance. Under Section 1950.5 of the California Civil Code, Landlord may withhold only that portion of Tenants' security deposit necessary to: (1) remedy any default by Tenants in the payment of rent; (2) repair damages to the premises exclusive of ordinary wear and tear; and (3) clean the premises if necessary.

OTHER WAYS TO HANDLE THE INITIAL RENT PAYMENT

There are several ways to pro-rate payments for tenants who move in mid-month:

1. Require the pro-rated rent of less than half a month plus the next month's entire rent. For example, a tenant who moves in on June 19 and pays $300 for the rent through June 30 should also be asked to pay in advance the $900 rent for July.

2. Insist on an entire month's rent up front and then pro-rate the second month. For example, the tenant who moves in on June 19 would first pay the full $900 rent. Then come July 1, the $300 rent for June 19 through 30 is due.

3. Instead of pro-rating, simply require rent payments on the day of the month that the tenant moved in, so that a tenant who moves in on the 19th will always pay rent on the 19th.

Clause 6. Late Charges

Late charges provide an incentive for tenants to pay rent on time and make sense when used with discretion. Unfortunately, landlords sometimes try to charge excessive late fees and, by so doing, get themselves into legal hot water and incur tenant hostility. Some California courts have ruled that contracts which provide for unreasonably high late charges are not enforceable.

Some cities with rent control ordinances regulate the amount of late fees. Check any rent control ordinances or regulations applicable to your property before establishing a late fee.

There are no statutory guidelines specifying what qualifies as a reasonable late fee. You should, however, be on safe ground and avoid legal problems if you adhere to these principles:

- It usually makes sense to voluntarily allow a grace period of at least a few days. Imposing a late charge if the rent is held up in the mail for a couple days won't endear you to your tenants.

- If you use a flat fee, it should not exceed 4% to 6% of the rent (for example, $30 to $45 on a $750-per-month rental). A late charge much higher than this (say, a 10% charge of $75 for being one day late with rent on a $750-per-month apartment) would probably not be upheld in court.

- If you add a late charge each day rent is late (say $5 or $10 per day), it should be moderate and have an upper limit. A reasonable cap is usually 4% to 6% of the rental amount. A late charge that increases without limit could be considered interest charged at a usurious rate. For example, an uncapped ten dollars a day on a $1,000 per month rent is 3,650% annual interest.

- Don't try to disguise excessive late charges by giving a "discount" for timely payment of rent. Giving a relatively large discount for paying rent on time is, in effect, the same as charging an excessive late fee.

After you've decided on a late charge policy, specify how many days you'll allow as a grace period—typically three or five. Next, fill in the late charge for the first day rent is late, followed by the amount for each additional day. Finally, fill in the maximum late charge.

Clause 7. Returned Check and Other Bank Charges

It's legal to charge the tenant an extra fee if a rent check bounces—assuming you agree to accept checks. (If you're having a lot of trouble with bounced checks, you may decide to change your agreement to accept only cash or money order payments for rent.) As with late charges, bounced check charges must be reasonable. You should charge no more than the amount your bank charges you for a returned check (such as $10 to $15 per returned item; check with your bank), plus a few dollars for your trouble.

In the blank, fill in the amount of the returned check charge. If you won't accept checks, fill in "N/A" or "Not applicable."

Clause 8. Amount and Payment of Deposits

It doesn't matter what term you use to define a security deposit; all have the same meaning as far as the law is concerned. By law, any "cleaning deposit," "cleaning fee," "security deposit" and "payment, fee, deposit, or charge," *including last month's rent* (but not first month's rent), paid by a tenant at the time she moves in, is a security deposit. (CC § 1950.5.) All of these deposits are subject to the laws that control the amounts and uses of security deposits.

Deposits Must Be Refundable

All security deposits must be refundable; it is illegal to collect nonrefundable fees or deposits. It's also illegal to charge a hidden nonrefundable deposit by charging considerably more rent for the first or last month than for other months. For example, you can't require tenants to pay a cleaning fee in addition to their last month's rent. It is similarly illegal to charge a fixed fee for cleaning drapes or carpets, or for painting.

Dollar Limits on Deposits

State law limits the amount you can collect as a deposit. (CC § 1950.5(c).) Here are the rules:

- **Unfurnished property.** The deposit, including any last month's rent, can't exceed two months' rent.

- **Furnished property.** The deposit, including any last month's rent, can't exceed three months' rent. Property is considered "furnished" if it contains essential furniture such as a bed in each bedroom, a couch or chairs for the living area, an eating table with chairs and a refrigerator and stove.

- **Cities with restrictions on deposits.** Some cities with rent control ordinances—as well as Santa Cruz and Watsonville, which don't have rent control—place restrictions on deposit amounts, often in the form of requiring that the tenant receive interest. (See the accompanying chart, "Cities Requiring Interest or Separate Accounts for Security Deposits," on pages 14 to 15.) Before attempting to set or raise a deposit in a rent-controlled city, be sure to obtain a copy of the rent control ordinance.

- **Waterbeds.** If the tenant has a waterbed, the maximum allowed deposit increases by half a month's rent. So, if a tenant has a waterbed, you can charge a total deposit (including last month's rent) of up to 2.5 times the monthly rent for unfurnished property and 3.5 times the monthly rent for furnished property. (CC § 1940.5(h).) (For more on waterbeds, see Clause 20: Waterbeds, page 21.)

Following are some examples of how security deposits are calculated.

Example 1: Mario charges $500 per month rent for a two-bedroom apartment. The apartment is unfurnished, so the most Mario can charge is two months' rent, or $1,000 total deposit. It makes no difference whether or not the deposit is divided into last month's rent, cleaning fee and so forth. In other words, if Mario charges a $200 cleaning deposit, a $300 security deposit and $500 last month's rent, he is within the law. Remember, the rent Mario collects for the first month's rent doesn't count as a security deposit.

Example 2: Lenora rents out a three-bedroom furnished house for $1,500 a month. Since total deposits on furnished property can legally be three times the monthly rent, Lenora can charge up to $4,500 for last month's rent and deposits. This is in addition to the first month's rent of $1,500 that Lenora can (and should) insist on before turning the property over to a tenant. Realistically, Lenora might not find any takers if she insists on receiving $4,500 in deposits plus the first month's rent, for a total of $6,000. In the case of furnished property, the market often keeps the practical limit on deposits lower than the maximum allowed by law.

WHY NOT TO MAKE LAST MONTH'S RENT PART OF DEPOSIT

It's a poor idea to use the term "last month's rent" when establishing a "deposit" requirement. The reason is that no matter what you call it, the total amount of the deposit you can require is limited by law. (See "Dollar Limits on Deposits," above.) But if you voluntarily call a portion of your deposit "last month's rent" you can only use it for that purpose.

For example, if you ask for two up-front payments (remember, the total must be within the dollar limits) from a tenant and call one last month's rent and the other a security deposit, you are legally bound to use the last month's rent portion for that purpose only—not to repair damage or pay cleaning charges. By contrast, if you require a security deposit and do not mention last month's rent, the tenant will have to pay the last month's rent when it comes due and then wait until after moving out to get the security deposit back. If the tenant has damaged the premises or failed to pay rent, you can hold onto the appropriate amount of the entire deposit.

Interest, Accounts and Recordkeeping on Deposits

In most localities, you don't have to pay tenants interest on deposits or put deposits in a separate bank account—unless you agree to this in your lease or rental agreement. In other words, you can simply put the money in your pocket, deposit in the bank or do anything else you want with it, as long as you have it available within three weeks of when the tenant moves out (effective 1/1/94). We've included a Security Deposit Itemization form for this purpose. For more information on security deposits and refunds, see Chapter 5 of *The Landlord's Law Book, Volume 1: Rights and Responsibilities*, by David Brown & Ralph Warner (Nolo Press).

Some landlords have found that it is good public relations to pay tenants interest on their deposits, even if there is no local law in requiring it. This, of course, is up to you.

Several cities, however, require landlords to pay or credit tenants with interest on security deposits. And a few cities require that security deposit funds be kept in separate interest-bearing accounts.

➡ These cities require landlords to pay interest on security deposits, or place other restrictions on security deposits: Berkeley, Cotati, East Palo Alto, Hayward, Los Angeles, San Francisco, Santa Cruz, Santa Monica, Watsonville and West Hollywood. If your property isn't located in one of these cities, skip to "Fill In Clause 8," page 14.

Here are a few things you should keep in mind about local requirements for interest payments on security deposits:

1. All cities that require landlords to pay interest on security deposits have rent control except Santa Cruz and Watsonville.
2. All cities that require landlords to pay tenants interest during the tenancy allow the landlord to either pay it directly to the tenant or credit it against the rent.
3. For those cities that require landlords to put deposits in separate accounts:
   - Only one account is required for all the landlord's deposits. You don't have to open one for each tenant's deposit.
   - All security deposits, including last month's rent, if collected, must be placed in the separate account.

The accompanying chart, "Cities Requiring Interest or Separate Accounts for Security Deposits," summarizes the features of all California cities' deposit laws. If you own property in a rent control city, and your property is exempt from rent control, these provisions do not apply. (See "Exceptions" for each city in the Rent Control Chart in Appendix 1.)

Fill In Clause 8

Once you've decided how much security deposit you can charge, fill in the amount in the blank. Then check either "a" or "b." Check "a" if your property is not located in a city that requires payment of interest. Or check "b" if interest payments must be made or credited, and summarize the requirement. You may copy the explanation from "Payments During Tenancy" in the accompanying chart.

CITIES REQUIRING INTEREST OR SEPARATE ACCOUNTS FOR SECURITY DEPOSITS

City	Ordinance	Interest-Bearing Account	Payments During Tenancy	Other Features
Berkeley	Rent Stabilization and Eviction for Good Cause Ordinance, § 7	Required. Account must be in a savings and loan insured by FSLIC (Federal Savings & Loan Insurance Corp.), or landlord must pay 10% annual interest.	All interest produced must be paid or credited in December of each year and when deposit refunded at end of tenancy.	
Cotati	Municipal Code §19.12.150	Required. Account must be "insured."	All interest produced must be paid when deposit refunded at end of tenancy.	
East Palo Alto	Ordinance 17-83, § 7	Required. Account must be insured by FSLIC, if account at savings and loan, or FDIC (Federal Deposit Insurance Corp.), if account at bank.	All interest produced must be paid in December of each year and when deposit refunded at end of tenancy.	
Hayward	Ordinance 83-023, § 13	Not required.	Landlord must pay interest on deposits held over a year, with payments made within 20 days of tenant's move-in "anniversary date" each year, and when deposit refunded at end of tenancy. Rate is set annually by city.	Violation can subject landlord to liability for three times the amount of unpaid interest owed.

(continued)

City	Ordinance	Interest-Bearing Account	Payments During Tenancy	Other Features
Los Angeles	Ordinance No. 166368	Not required.	Landlord must pay 5% annual interest rate on deposits held over a year. Payments need only be made every five years and when deposit refunded at end of tenancy. (Interest requirement is not being enforced pending legal challenge. See Appendix 1: Rent Control Chart.)	
San Francisco	Administrative Code, Chapter 49. (Not part of city's rent control law.)	Not required.	Landlord must pay 5% annual interest on deposits held over a year with payments made on tenant's move-in "anniversary date" each year, and when deposit refunded at end of tenancy.	Ordinance does not apply to government-subsidized housing but may apply in other situations, even though property not subject to rent control.
Santa Cruz	Municipal Code §§ 21.02.010-21.02.090	Not required.	Landlord must pay 2.5% annual interest rate on deposits held over a year, with payments made on tenant's move-in "anniversary date" each year, and when deposit refunded at end of tenancy.	Santa Cruz has no rent control law.
Santa Monica	City Charter Article XV111, Chapter 14	Required. Account must be insured by FSLIC or FDIC.	Landlord need not pay tenant any of the interest, but failure to do so is a "factor" in the city denying an individual landlord's requested rent increase (or granting a tenant's requested rent decrease).	Landlord cannot raise deposit during tenancy, even if rent is raised, unless tenant agrees.
Watsonville	Municipal Code §§ 5.40.01-5.40.08	Not required	On deposits held over six months, landlord must pay interest or credit against rent. Payment or rent credit is due on January 1st and when deposit is refunded at end of tenancy. Rate is set annually by city.	Watsonville has no rent control law.
West Hollywood	Municipal Code Section 6408(B)	Not required.	Landlord must pay interest on deposits, with payments made or credited against rent in January or February of each year, and when deposit refunded at end of tenancy. Rate is set annually by city.	

Clause 9. Utilities

This clause helps prevent misunderstandings. Normally, landlords pay for garbage (and sometimes water, if there is a yard) to help make sure that the premises are well-maintained. Tenants usually pay for other services, such as phone, gas and electricity. In the blank, fill in the utilities you—not the tenants—will be responsible for paying. If you'll pay all or a portion of the utilities, indicate that—for example, "all utilities except phone" or "half of the electricity and half of the gas." If the tenant will pay all utilities, fill in "N/A" or "Not Applicable."

If there are not separate gas and electric meters for each unit, and a tenant's meter serves any areas outside her control (even a light bulb not under the tenant's control in a common area), you must disclose these facts before the tenant moves in. (CC § 1940.9.)

 If your rental property does not have shared utility arrangements, skip to Clause 10.

If your rental property has shared utility arrangements, check the box and copy only one of the two options provided below.

Option 1: "Landlord will pay for the utilities for the Tenants' meter, and will place that utility in Landlord's own name."

Option 2: "Tenants will pay for gas and electricity charged to their meter, with the understanding that they may be paying for others' utility charges."

If at all possible, avoid having the tenant pay for others' utilities. Regardless of how few dollars a month a tenant may be paying for another tenant's or the landlord's common-area utilities, a tenant faced with this sort of uncertainty will usually demand a concession on rent; this will probably cost you more in the long run than if you simply paid for the utilities yourself, or perhaps added a new meter.

Clause 10. Prohibition of Assignment and Subletting

The lease and rental agreement forbid sublets or assignments without the owner's written consent.

Subletting consists of a tenant renting all or part of the property to another person, the subtenant. A subtenant does not sign a rental agreement or lease with the landlord. The tenant who moves out temporarily—for the summer, for example—may sublet an entire dwelling to a subtenant. Or, a subtenant may rent one or more rooms from the tenant, who continues to live in the unit.

In effect, the tenant functions as the subtenant's landlord. The subtenant is responsible to the tenant for whatever rent they've agreed on between themselves. The tenant, in turn, is responsible to the landlord for the rent.

If a tenant permanently gives his or her right to live in the premises to another person, it's called an **assignment**, because the tenant has legally assigned all his or her rights to someone else. The new occupant is responsible to the landlord for everything the original tenant was liable for—even without an agreement between the assignee and the landlord. (CC § 822.) (The previous occupant remains liable to the landlord also, unless the landlord agrees otherwise in writing.)

This clause is designed to prevent your tenant from subletting or assigning the lease or rental agreement without your consent. By including this clause in your agreement, you have the option not to accept a sublet or assignment if you don't like or trust the person your tenant proposes to take over the lease.

You don't need to add anything to this clause.

If a tenant breaks a lease, you still have a duty to limit damages. If a tenant with a lease leaves early, you have the duty to try and re-rent the premises. Assuming you can, the money you receive from the new tenant must be subtracted from what the first tenant owes for the rest of the lease, as part of determining whether and how much the first tenant still owes. Knowing this, many a tenant who breaks a lease may provide you with another suitable tenant. If this occurs, the first tenant is off the financial hook, whether or not you choose to refuse to rent to the second tenant.

Clause 11. Condition of the Premises

This clause makes it clear that if the tenants damage the premises—for example, break a window or scratch hardwood floors—it's their responsibility to pay for fixing the problem. It also explains that the tenants agree to notify you immediately if there are any repairs that need to be made. To protect your property, you should establish clear, easy-to-follow procedures for your tenants to ask for repairs. This kit includes a self-explanatory Maintenance/Repair Request form for Tenants to report defects and safety problems. You should respond quickly when requests are made and make regular safety inspections of the premises to check for hazardous conditions.

In the blanks after the words, "except as noted here," clearly describe any defects or damages to the premises. If there are none, state that. You and your tenants may find it easiest to go through the rental unit before the tenants move in and fill out a Landlord/Tenant Checklist, provided

Landlord shall pay Tenants interest on all security deposits as follows:

☒ a. Under local law, no interest payments are required.

☐ b. Local law requires that interest be paid or credited, which shall occur as follows:

_____

9. **Utilities.** Tenants shall be responsible for payment of all utility charges, except for the following, which shall be paid by Landlord:
       _garbage and water_____

☐ Tenants' gas or electric meter serves area(s) outside of their premises and there are not separate gas and electric meters for Tenants' unit and the area(s) outside their unit. Tenants and Landlord agree as follows:

_____

10. **Prohibition of Assignment and Subletting.** Tenants shall not sublet any part of the premises or assign this Agreement without the prior written consent of Landlord.

11. **Condition of the Premises.** Tenants agree to: (1) keep the premises clean and sanitary and in good repair and, upon termination of the tenancy, to return the premises to Landlord in a condition identical to that which existed when Tenants took occupancy, except for ordinary wear and tear; (2) immediately notify Landlord of any defects or dangerous conditions in and about the premises of which they become aware; and (3) reimburse Landlord, on demand by Landlord, for the cost of any repairs to the premises damaged by Tenants or their guests or invitees through misuse or neglect.

    Tenants acknowledge that they have examined the premises, including appliances, fixtures, carpets, drapes and paint, and have found them to be in good, safe and clean condition and repair, except as noted here:

_____
_____
_____
_____

12. **Possession of the Premises.** If, after signing this Agreement, Tenants fail to take possession of the premises, they shall still be responsible for paying rent and complying with all other terms of this Agreement. In the event Landlord is unable to deliver possession of the premises to Tenants for any reason not within Landlord's control, including, but not limited to, failure of prior occupants to vacate or partial or complete destruction of the premises, Tenants shall have the right to terminate this Agreement. In such event, Landlord's liability to Tenants shall be limited to the return of all sums previously paid by Tenants to Landlord.

13. **Pets.** No animal, bird or other pet shall be kept on the premises without Landlord's prior written consent, except properly trained dogs needed by blind, deaf or physically disabled persons and:

    ☐ a. None.

    ☒ b. _one cat_____, under the following conditions:
    _____

14. **Landlord's Access for Inspection and Emergency.** Landlord or Landlord's agents may enter the premises in the event of an emergency to make repairs or improvements, supply agreed services and show the premises to prospective buyers or tenants. Except in cases of emergency, Tenants' abandonment of the premises or court order, Landlord shall give Tenants reasonable notice of intent to enter and shall enter only during regular business hours of Monday through Friday from 9:00 a.m. to 6:00 p.m. and Saturday from 10:00 a.m. to 1:00 p.m.

in this kit and discussed on page 31. That simple form describes what is in the rental unit and specifies its condition. If you decide to use the checklist, fill in the words, "See Landlord/Tenant Checklist attached."

⚠️ **If you fail to maintain the property:** If your tenants or their guests suffer injury or property damage as a result of poorly-maintained property, you may be held responsible for paying for the loss.

Clause 12. Possession of the Premises

This clause explains that if the tenants choose not to move in after they have signed a lease or rental agreement, they will still be required to pay rent and satisfy other conditions of the lease or rental agreement.

This clause also protects you if you're unable, for reasons beyond your control, to turn over possession after having signed the agreement. You don't need to add anything.

Clause 13. Pets

This clause is designed to prevent tenants from keeping pets without your written permission. Without this sort of provision, particularly in a fixed-term lease that can't be terminated on 30 days' notice, there's little to prevent your tenant from keeping dangerous or non-housebroken pets on your property, except for city ordinances prohibiting tigers and the like.

You have the right to prohibit all pets, with the exception of trained dogs used by blind, deaf or physically handicapped people. You may not charge an extra pet deposit on account of any trained dog. (CC §§ 54.1, 54.2.)

Check "a" if you want to forbid pets.

Or, to allow pets, check "b" and identify the type and number of pets—for example, "one cat." If you allow pets, you're wise to spell out your pet rules—for example, you may want to specify that the tenants will keep the yard free of all animal waste. You may also want to charge a higher security deposit, if you aren't already requiring the maximum allowed by law.

⚠️ **Enforce no-pets clauses.** When faced with tenants who violate no-pets clauses, landlords sometimes ignore the situation for a long time, then try to enforce the clause later if friction develops over some other matter. This could backfire. In general, a landlord who knows a tenant has breached the lease or rental agreement by keeping a pet, and does nothing about it for a long time, may have implicitly waived the right to object. So, if you want to keep your rental units pet free, state your policy in the lease or rental agreement and enforce it.

SECURITY DEPOSITS AND PETS

Some landlords allow pets, but require the tenant to pay a separate deposit to cover any damages caused by the pet. This is legal only if the pet deposit, when added to the amount charged for the security deposit, does not exceed the maximum security deposit amount. (See "Clause 8: Amount and Payment of Deposits," page 12.)

Separate pet deposits are usually a bad idea because they limit how you can use that part of the security deposit. For example, if the pet is well-behaved, but the tenant trashes your unit, you can't use the pet portion of the deposit to clean up after the human. If you want to protect your property from damage done by a pet, you are probably better off charging a slightly higher rent or security deposit to start with (assuming you are not restricted by rent control or the upper security deposit limits).

Clause 14. Landlord's Access for Inspection and Emergency

By law, you as a landlord have a legal right of access to the property to make repairs or show the premises for sale or rental, provided you give the tenant reasonable notice, which is presumed to be 24 hours. This clause defines "ordinary business hours" to include weekdays and part of Saturday.

You don't need to add anything to this clause.

⚠️ **Ordinary business hours not established by law:** The law does not specify exactly what are "ordinary business hours." A tenant could, for example, object to your entering the premises on a Saturday morning. Common sense suggests that you be considerate of your tenants and do your best to accommodate their schedules.

Clause 15. Extended Absences By Tenants

This clause requires that the tenants notify you when leaving your property for an extended time.

In the blank, fill in the time frame that you'd like to be notified of. Fourteen days is common, but you may opt for an altogether different period of time. For example, if you

15. **Extended Absences By Tenants.** Tenants agree to notify Landlord in the event that they will be away from the premises for __10__ consecutive days or more. During such absence, Landlord may enter the premises at times reasonably necessary to maintain the property and inspect for damage and needed repairs.

16. **Prohibitions Against Violating Laws and Causing Disturbances.** Tenants shall be entitled to quiet enjoyment of the premises. Tenants and their guests or invitees shall not use the premises or adjacent areas in such a way as to: (1) violate any law or ordinance, including laws prohibiting the use, possession or sale of illegal drugs; (2) commit waste or nuisance; or (3) annoy, disturb, inconvenience or interfere with the quiet enjoyment and peace and quiet of any other tenant or nearby resident.

17. **Repairs and Alterations**
    a. Tenants shall not, without Landlord's prior written consent, alter, re-key or install any locks to the premises or install or alter any burglar alarm system. Tenants shall provide Landlord with a key or keys capable of unlocking all such re-keyed or new locks as well as instructions on how to disarm any altered or new burglar alarm system.
    b. Except as provided by law or as authorized by the prior written consent of Landlord, Tenants shall not make any repairs or alterations to the premises.
    ❏ Landlord and Tenants agree to the following:
    _____
    _____
    _____

18. **Damage to the Premises.** In the event the premises are partially or totally damaged or destroyed by fire or other cause, the following shall apply:
    a. If the premises are totally damaged and destroyed, Landlord shall have the option to: (1) repair such damage and restore the premises, with this Agreement continuing in full force and effect, except that Tenants' rent shall be abated while repairs are being made; or (2) give written notice to Tenants terminating this Agreement at any time within thirty (30) days after such damage, and specifying the termination date; in the event that Landlord gives such notice, this Agreement shall expire and all of Tenants' rights pursuant to this Agreement shall cease.
    b. Landlord shall have the option to determine that the premises are only partially damaged by fire or other cause. In that event, Landlord shall attempt to repair such damage and restore the premises within thirty (30) days after such damage. If only part of the premises cannot be used, Tenants must pay rent only for the usable part, to be determined solely by Landlord. If Landlord is unable to complete repairs within thirty (30) days, this Agreement shall expire and all of Tenants' rights pursuant to this Agreement shall terminate at the option of either party.
    c. In the event that Tenants, or their guests or invitees, in any way caused or contributed to the damage of the premises, Landlord shall have the right to terminate this Agreement at any time, and Tenants shall be responsible for all losses, including, but not limited to, damage and repair costs as well as loss of rental income.
    d. Landlord shall not be required to repair or replace any property brought onto the premises by Tenants.

19. **Tenants' Financial Responsibility and Renters' Insurance.** Tenants agree to accept financial responsibility for any loss or damage to personal property belonging to Tenants and their guests and invitees caused by theft, fire or any other cause. Landlord assumes no liability for any such loss. Landlord recommends that Tenants obtain a renter's insurance policy from a recognized insurance firm to cover Tenants' liability, personal property damage and damage to the premises.

20. **Waterbeds.** No waterbed or other item of water-filled furniture shall be kept on the premises without Landlord's written consent.
    ☒ Landlord grants Tenants permission to keep water-filled furniture on the premises. Attachment __1__: Agreement Regarding Use of Waterbed is attached to and incorporated into this Agreement by reference.

live in Truckee or Mt. Shasta, checking your property on a daily basis during the winter may be prudent, to make sure the pipes haven't burst.

Clause 16. Prohibitions Against Violating Laws and Causing Disturbances

This type of clause is found in most form leases and rental agreements. Although it's full of legal gobbledygook, it's probably best to leave it as is, since courts have much experience in working with these terms. If the tenant causes a nuisance, seriously damages the property or violates the law—for example, deals drugs—you may be able to evict him even without such a provision in the agreement. It will, however, be easier to evict if you can point to an explicit lease provision. If you want to add specific rules—for example, no loud music played after midnight—add them to Clause 24: Additional Provisions, page 22. (Waste and nuisance are defined below.)

WASTE AND NUISANCE: WHAT ARE THEY?

In legalese, **waste** is the causing of severe property damage to real estate, including a house or apartment unit, which goes way beyond ordinary wear and tear. Punching holes in walls, pulling out sinks and fixtures and knocking down doors are examples of "committing waste."

Nuisance refers to behavior that prevents neighbors from fully enjoying the use of their own homes. Continuous loud noise and foul odors are examples of legal nuisances that may disturb nearby neighbors.

Clause 17. Repairs and Alterations

The first part of this clause forbids the tenant from rekeying the locks or installing a burglar alarm system without your consent, and provides that you are entitled to duplicate keys and instructions on how to disarm the alarm system.

The "except as provided by law" language is a reference to the "repair-and-deduct" remedy the tenants may use to repair health- or safety-threatening defects. By law, landlords must maintain and repair their rental property in accordance with certain minimum standards. (CC § 1941.1.) If a landlord refuses to do so, after reasonable notification by the tenant, a tenant may arrange for certain repairs and deduct the cost from the next month's rent. (CC § 1942.) The tenant always has the right to use this statutory procedure, no matter what a lease says. If a landlord doesn't keep the property in habitable condition, tenants may have the right to withhold rent and even sue.

If mutually agreeable to you and the tenants, they may agree in writing to perform necessary repairs or maintenance in exchange for a rent reduction. (For more information, see *The Landlord's Law Book, Volume 1: Rights and Responsibilities*, by David Brown & Ralph Warner (Nolo Press).)

This clause makes it clear that alterations and repairs without the landlord's written consent aren't allowed. If you wish, you may check the box and authorize (or prohibit) certain repairs or alterations. For example, you may want to prohibit the use of nails or tacks in the walls, or you may want to allow the tenants to paint the walls. Either fill in the blank lines or add an Attachment page. (See "How To Prepare Attachment Pages," on page 29.)

If you grant written permission to install a bookshelf, security system, kitchen cupboards screwed to studs or anything that is firmly attached to your property, make sure that you and the tenant are clear about whether or not the fixture is to remain in place when she leaves. By law, things permanently attached to your property by nails or screws are called "fixtures." (Fixtures are completely defined in CC § 1019.) Fixtures belong to you except where "the removal can be affected without injury to the premises," unless you permit their removal. To avoid confusion later, it makes sense for you and the tenant to agree whether any fixture a tenant installs can be removed and if so, if there are any conditions accompanying the removal.

> **Example 1:** "Tenants have permission to install a set of bookshelves by use of four-inch screws attached to the wall studs of the long wall of the rear bedroom of the premises. Tenants acknowledge and understands that the bookshelves, once installed, are to be considered part of the premises, and are not to be removed when their tenancy ends."
>
> **Example 2:** "Tenants may install a rotating fan in the light fixture in the master bedroom. When Tenants move out of the premises, they shall remove the fan and return the light fixture to its original condition."

Clause 18. Damage to Premises

This clause addresses what would happen if the premises are seriously damaged by fire or other calamity. This provision places responsibility on Tenants for damage caused by their acts or by people they've allowed in the premises. Basically, it seeks to limit your risk to thirty days' rental value, even if the damage was your responsibility. You don't need to add anything to this clause.

Clause 19. Tenants' Financial Responsibility and Renters' Insurance

This clause forces the tenants to assume responsibility for damage to their own belongings. It also suggests that tenants obtain renters' insurance.

Clause 20. Waterbeds

Whether or not you can refuse to rent to a tenant with a waterbed depends on when the property was built. Here are the rules:

- **Property built before January 1, 1973.** You have the right to refuse to allow a tenant to have a waterbed, and you may choose not to rent to a prospective tenant on the basis that he or she has a waterbed. When making your decision, bear in mind that wooden floors built to the standards of 20 or 30 years ago can withstand pressures of at least 60 pounds per square foot, and a typical queen-sized waterbed exerts about 50 pounds per square foot. Poured concrete floors, of course, pose no problem.

- **Property built on or after January 1, 1973.** By law, you cannot refuse to rent to a tenant simply because he or she has a waterbed. Nor can you refuse to renew a lease for the reason that the tenant has a waterbed. (CC § 1940.5.) However, you may—and should—insist on strict standards regarding the installation and construction of the waterbed.

If your property was built before 1973 and you wish to ban waterbeds, you may cross off the words "without Landlord's written consent."

If you choose to allow waterbeds, or your property was built in 1973 or later and your tenant plans to have a waterbed, check the box and complete the self-explanatory fill-in-the-blanks Attachment: Agreement Regarding Use of Waterbed, which is provided in this kit. Remember to fill in the number of the attachment. (See "How To Prepare Attachment Pages," on page 29 for information.)

> ⚠ **Security deposits may be increased:** You may charge a higher security deposit for tenants with waterbeds, equal to an additional one-half month's rent. (See Clause 8: Amount and Payment of Deposits, page 12.)

Clause 21. Tenant Rules and Regulations

Many landlords don't worry about detailed rules and regulations, especially when they rent single-family homes or duplexes. However, in large buildings, rules are usually important to control the use of common areas and equipment.

Check the box if you plan to use tenant rules and fill in the attachment number. Remember to label the rules and regulations with the attachment number. This clause gives you the authority to evict a tenant who persists in seriously violating your code of tenant rules and regulations.

WHAT'S COVERED IN TENANT RULES AND REGULATIONS

Tenant rules and regulations typically cover issues such as:

- elevator safety and use
- pool rules
- parking garage regulations
- lock-out charges
- security system use
- excessive noise
- pets
- use of grounds
- maintenance of balconies and decks (for instance, no drying clothes on balconies)
- display of signs in windows, and
- laundry room rules.

Clause 22. Payment of Attorney Fees in a Lawsuit

Many landlords wrongly assume that whenever they sue a tenant and win, the court will order the losing tenant to pay the landlord's attorney fees. However, this is true only if a written agreement specifically provides for it. This is why it can be important to have an "attorney fees" clause in your lease. That way, if you hire a lawyer to bring an eviction suit and win, the judge will order your tenant to pay your attorney fees.

By law, an attorney fees clause in a lease or rental agreement works both ways. (CC § 1717.) That is, if your tenants prevail in a lawsuit, and the lease or written rental agreement contains such a clause, you must pay their "reasonable attorney fees," in an amount determined by the judge. This is true even if the clause is worded so that it requires payment of attorney fees only by the tenant if you win and not vice-versa.

> ⚠ **Maybe you don't want to provide for attorney fees:** Some landlords choose not to allow for attorney fees because of their experience that money judgments against evicted tenants are very often uncollectible, so that in practice, the clause does not help the landlord. And, such a clause may hurt him, because it works both ways—if the landlord loses a lawsuit, she'll have to pay the tenant's attorney fees, and that judgment *will* be collectible.

If you intend to do your own legal work in any potential eviction or other lawsuit, even if the tenant hires a lawyer, you will almost surely conclude that it is wiser not to allow for attorney fees. You don't want to be in a situation where you'd have to pay the tenant's attorney fees if she won, but she wouldn't have to pay yours if you won because you didn't hire a lawyer.

If you don't want to allow for attorney fees, check the first box before the words "shall not."

If you want to be entitled to attorney fees if you win—and you're willing to pay attorney fees if you lose—check the second box before the words "shall recover."

Clause 23. Authority to Receive Legal Papers

By law, you must give your tenants information about everyone who is authorized to receive notices and legal papers, such as lawsuits from the tenants. (CC §§1961-1962.7.) For this purpose, you must provide the name and street address of:

- the manager, if any, and
- an owner, or someone else you authorize to receive notices and legal papers on your behalf.

a. Check "a" if you have a manager, and fill in his or her name and address in the blanks.

b. Check "b" if you want to receive legal notices yourself, and fill in your name and street address.

c. Check "c" if you wish to designate someone else to receive legal papers on your behalf. Then fill in that person's name and address in the blanks.

> ⚠ **Do You Trust Your Manager?** It's unwise to have a manager whom you wouldn't trust to receive legal papers on your behalf. You don't, for example, want a flaky apartment manager to throw away notice of a lawsuit against you without informing you. That could result in a judgment against you and a lien against your property in a lawsuit you didn't even know about. (For more information on using property managers, see Chapter 6 of *The Landlord's Law Book, Volume 1: Rights and Responsibilities,* by David Brown & Ralph Warner (Nolo Press).)

Clause 24. Additional Provisions

In this clause, you may fill in any additional provisions you want to address in the lease or rental agreement.

a. If there are no additional provisions, check "a."

b. If you want to include any additional clauses in your lease or rental agreement, check "b."

If you need to add extensive provisions to the lease or rental agreement, add Attachment pages as needed. (See "How To Prepare Attachment Pages," page 29.)

ADDITIONAL PROVISIONS YOU MAY WANT TO ADD

Some landlords find it helpful to spell out exactly how they expect their tenants to take care of the premises. Here are some key areas:

- **smoke detectors (frequency for checking and replacing batteries):** "Tenants agree to test all smoke detectors at least once a month and to report any problems to Landlord in writing. Tenants agree to replace all smoke detector batteries as necessary."

- **yard work, snow shoveling and other maintenance:** "Tenants agree to regularly water and maintain the grounds, including lawn, shrubbery and flowers."

- **rules for taking care of furniture or other items on the premises:** "Tenants will keep the hot tub covered when not in use. Tenants will use and clean the hot tub regularly, according to the manufacturer's instructions attached to this Agreement as Attachment 1."

Clause 25. Entire Agreement

This provision protects you from liability for anything a tenant claims you promised orally. It also works the other way: If a tenant with a written rental agreement or lease makes oral promises—such as paying extra rent if another person moves in—and doesn't do so, you aren't covered because the promises weren't written down.

Get everything you want included in your rental agreement in writing before you sign. Any agreements made later should be done in writing in the form of an amendment. You may use the self-explanatory Amendment to Lease or Rental Agreement form provided in this kit.

Finally, this clause states that any violation of the Agreement by tenants or people they let in the premises is terms for ending the tenancy.

21. Tenant Rules and Regulations

☒ Tenants acknowledge receipt of, and have read a copy of, tenant rules and regulations, which are labeled Attachment __2__ and attached to and incorporated into this Agreement by reference.

22. Payment of Attorney Fees in a Lawsuit. In any action or legal proceeding to enforce any part of this Agreement, the prevailing party ☒ shall not/ ☐ shall recover reasonable attorney fees and court costs.

23. Authority to Receive Legal Papers. Any person managing the premises, the owner and anyone designated by the owner are authorized to accept service of process and receive other notices and demands, which may be delivered to:

☐ a. The manager, at the following address: _____

☒ b. The owner, at the following address: _125 Sendaro Street, Fresno, California 93656_

☐ c. The following: _____

24. Additional Provisions

☒ a. None

☐ b. Additional provisions are as follows:

25. Entire Agreement. This document constitutes the entire Agreement between the parties, and no promises or representations, other than those contained here and those implied by law, have been made by Landlord or Tenants. Any modifications to this Agreement must be in writing signed by Landlord and Tenants. The failure of Tenants or their guests or invitees to comply with any term of this Agreement is grounds for termination of the tenancy, with appropriate notice to tenants and procedures as required by law.

Lionel Jones   11/14/9X
Landlord/Manager   Date

125 Sendaro Street, Fresno, California 93656
Landlord/Manager's Street Address, City, State & Zip

Sharon Donaldson   11/14/9X
Tenant   Date

Hank Donaldson   11/14/9X
Tenant   Date

_____   _____
Tenant   Date

FINDING SUITABLE TENANTS

All landlords typically follow the same process when renting property:

Step 1. Decide on rental terms, including amounts of rent and deposits and the length of the tenancy.

Step 2. Advertise the property.

Step 3. Accept all applications.

Step 4. Screen potential tenants.

Step 5. Choose someone to rent the property.

Step 6. Provide disclosures if the property is located near a former military base or contains asbestos.

Step 7. Cash rent and security deposit checks before the tenant moves in.

Step 1: Decide on Terms of the Rental

By preparing a draft of your lease or rental agreement, you've already made the key decisions necessary to rent your property, such as how much rent to charge and how large of a security deposit to require. You're certainly free to modify those choices, as long as you stay within the law.

Always be consistent when dealing with prospective tenants. The reason for this is simple: If you don't treat all tenants more or less equally—for example, if you arbitrarily set tougher standards for renting to a racial minority, woman or family with children—you can easily be accused of discriminatory conduct.

Be sure all prospective tenants know all your general requirements before you get too far in the process. (For more detailed information on discrimination and rentals, see *The Landlord's Law Book, Volume 1: Rights and Responsibilities,* by David Brown & Ralph Warner (Nolo Press).)

> **Don't skip decision-making:** Instructions in this kit for filling in leases and rental agreements explain your legal obligations when renting property. Follow the instructions in "Fill In a Draft Lease or Rental Agreement Form," beginning on page 7, *before* you advertise your property, screen applicants or offer your property for rent.

Step 2: Advertise the Property

> **If you have tenants lined up:** If you've already advertised or were lucky enough to fill your vacancy by word-of-mouth, skip to "Step 6: Provide Disclosures if Required By Law," page 27.

There is one crucial point you should remember about advertising: Where you advertise is more important than how you advertise. For example, if you rent primarily to college students, your best bet is the campus newspaper or housing office, not a metropolitan newspaper. In short, whether you simply put a sign in front of your apartment building or work with a rental service, advertise in such a way that you reach a sufficient number of potential tenants.

Legally, you should have no trouble if you follow these simple rules:

Make sure the price in your ad is an honest one. If a tenant shows up promptly and agrees to all the terms set out in your ad, you may run afoul of the law if you arbitrarily raise the price, especially if this can be construed as illegal discrimination. This doesn't mean you are always legally required to rent at your advertised price, however. If a tenant asks for more services or different lease terms, which you feel require more rent (for example, you list the unit for two, but three roommates want to rent it), it's fine to bargain and raise your price. However, be sure to abide by applicable rent limits set by any local rent control ordinance.

Don't engage in bait-and-switch tactics by advertising something you don't have. Some large landlords, management companies and rental services have advertised units that weren't really available in order to produce a large number of prospective tenants who could then be "switched" to higher priced or inferior units. This type of advertising is illegal, and many property owners have been prosecuted for bait-and-switch practices.

Be sure your ad can't be construed as discriminatory. Ads should not mention age, sex, race, religion, disability or adults-only, unless yours is senior citizen housing. (If so, it must comply with rules set out in CC § 51.3—namely, it must be reserved for persons over age 62, or be a complex of 150 or more units (35 in non-metropolitan areas) for persons over age 55.) Ads should not imply through words, photographs or illustrations that you prefer or discriminate against renters because of group characteristics such as their age, sex, race, etc. In addition, discrimination that is unrelated to a legitimate landlord concern is illegal. For example, it's discriminatory to refuse to rent to students who otherwise qualify as suitable tenants.

It is an excellent idea to state in your ads that you provide "equal opportunity housing" or something similar, just as most businesses routinely include this statement in employment ads.

> **Example:** An ad for an apartment that says, "Young, female student preferred" is illegal, since sex and age discrimination are forbidden by both state and federal law. Under California law, discrimination based on the prospective tenant's occupation also is illegal, since there is no legitimate business reason to prefer tenants with certain occupations over others.

Try to put legal and nondiscriminatory rules, such as no pets, in your ad. You can save yourself time screening out tenants you don't want by stating "no pets," "no smoking" or other rules in your ad. The wording of your ad does not, however, legally obligate you to rent on any particular terms. For example, if your ad doesn't specify "no pets," you certainly are not obligated to rent to someone with two Dobermans.

Step 3: Accept All Applications

Complete the box at the top of the Rental Application provided in this kit, listing the property address and amounts due before the tenants may move in.

If you intend to charge a credit-check fee, it should be reasonably related to the cost of the credit check—$10 to $20 is common. You may want to collect the credit-check fee at the time you take an individual's rental application. If, however, you expect a large number of applicants, you'd be wise not to accept credit-check fees. Instead, you'd probably want to read over the applications first and only do a credit check on applicants you're seriously considering. Any credit-check fees you don't use for that purpose must be returned.

The Rental Application form includes the amount and purpose of the credit-check charge. If you do not charge credit-check fees, simply fill in "none" or "N/A" at the bottom of the second page of the form. Otherwise, fill in the amount.

Ask all applicants to fill out a Rental Application form and accept applications from *everyone* who's interested in your rental property. Refusing to take an application may unnecessarily anger a prospective tenant, and will make him or her more likely to look into the possibility of filing a discrimination complaint. Make decisions about who will rent the property later. Each prospective tenant age 18 or older who wants to live in your rental property should fill out a written application. This is true whether you're renting to a married couple sharing an apartment or a number of unrelated roommates.

Always make sure that prospective tenants complete the entire Rental Application, including Social Security number, current employment and emergency contacts. You may need this information later to track down a tenant who skips town leaving unpaid rent or abandoned property.

Step 4: Screen Potential Tenants

If an application looks good, there are several ways to screen prospective tenants, depending on how thorough you want to be. Obviously, you want tenants who pay their bills on time and consistently. At the very least, you should always make a few phone calls to check references from the previous landlord and to verify income and employment. It's also wise to check the applicant's credit with one of the major credit reporting agencies. You may want to go further—for example, to check whether eviction suits have ever been filed against a prospective tenant.

> **Be consistent in your screening:** It may be considered discriminatory to call previous landlords of certain categories of applicants (for example, African-American applicants) but not others (for example, Asian-American applicants), or to require credit reports only from applicants of certain ethnic or racial groups.

Here are various ways to screen applicants, beginning with the most basic steps:

Check with previous landlords or managers given as references. The key questions to ask include:

- Did the tenant pay rent on time?
- Was the tenant considerate of neighbors—that is, no loud parties or music?
- If the tenant had pets, were they well-behaved?
- Did the tenant make any unreasonable demands or complaints?
- Why did the tenant leave?
- Did the tenant leave the place in good condition?

Make sure you speak to a legitimate landlord or manager, not a friend of the prospective tenant posing as one. Bad tenants often provide phony references. One suggestion is to call the number given for the previous landlord or manager and simply ask for the tenant by name, rather than begin by saying that you are checking references. If the prospective tenant has given you a friend's name, the friend will probably say something that gives away the scam.

If you still have questions, consider driving to the former address and checking things out in person. Finally, if you have any doubts, ask the previous landlord or manager to pull out the tenant's rental application so you can verify certain facts, such as the tenant's Social Security number. If the so-called landlord can't do this, it may be a sign that you are being conned.

Verify a potential tenant's income and employment. You want to make sure that all tenants have the income to pay the rent each month. Call the prospective tenant's employer to verify income and length of employment. Some employers require written authorization from the employee; this is included at the bottom of our Rental Application form.

If you feel that verifying an individual's income by telephone, or accepting a note from her boss, is not reliable enough, you may require applicants to provide copies of recent paycheck stubs. It's also reasonable to require documentation of other sources of income (such as checks for disability or other benefits). Where a large portion of an applicant's income is from child support or alimony payments, you might want to ask for a copy of the court decree for the support payments. However, don't go overboard by asking for copies of tax returns or bank statements, except possibly from self-employed persons.

Obtain a credit report from a private credit reporting agency. Many landlords find it essential to check a tenant's credit history with at least one credit reporting agency. It's not uncommon to hear about near-horror stories in which a misguided landlord would have rented to a tenant from hell, but a credit report saved the day. Because the applicant—not you—will pay for the credit applicant check, you won't be risking anything other than a little time.

It is legal to charge prospective tenants a fee (say $10 to $20) for the cost of the credit report itself and your time and trouble. Our Rental Application alerts prospective tenants of this fee. Be warned, though: It is not legal to charge a credit check fee if you do not use it for the stated purpose and you pocket it instead.

If you own many rental properties and need credit reports frequently, consider joining one of the three largest credit reporting agencies—Equifax, Trans Union or TRW—which may charge $40-$50 in annual fees plus $5-$10 per report. You can find their numbers and those of other companies that do tenant screening in the yellow pages of the phone book under "Credit Reporting Agencies." Or, if you only rent a few units each year, see if your local apartment association (there are about two dozen in California) offers credit reporting services. With some credit reporting agencies, you can obtain a verbal credit report the same day it's requested, and a written one within a day or two.

If negative information in a credit report makes you decide not to rent or to charge higher rent to someone, you must so notify the applicant, and provide the name and address of the agency that reported the negative information. You must also tell the applicant that he has a right to obtain a copy of his file from the agency that reported the negative information, as long as he requests the file within 60 days. (CC § 1785.20.)

Companies legally may only report eviction cases that the landlord has won in court, unless the tenant signed a written settlement agreement allowing the case to be reported. (CC §§ 1785.13(a)(3), 1786.18(a)(4).) Tenants usually don't win eviction suits. In most cases, the tenant fails to respond to the suit and is evicted, or appears and loses after a court hearing.

As with credit-reporting agencies, if you don't rent to an applicant or charge more rent because of information from a tenant-reporting service, you must notify the applicant. Inform the applicant in writing of the nature of the report and give the name and address of the company.

Check with the applicant's bank to verify account information. If an individual's credit history raises questions of his or her financial stability, you may want to take this additional step. Banks differ as to the type of information they will provide over the phone. Generally, banks will at most only provide information as to average account balances and bad checks, if any. You may need to submit the applicant's written authorization, which is provided at the bottom of the Rental Application.

Be wary of an applicant who has no checking or savings account. It could be because the individual bounced so many checks her bank dropped her.

See if any "tenant-reporting services" operate in your area. Just as regular credit-reporting agencies keep tabs on retail purchasers' credit worthiness, businesses such as UD Registry of Van Nuys keep tabs on eviction suits (called unlawful detainer, hence the "UD") against tenants. Your local apartment association may recommend other services of this type. Tenant-reporting services typically charge from $20 to $50.

Step 5: Select the Tenants

Once you have several applications, make your selection. Assuming you choose the candidate with the best qualifications to be a tenant (job, credit history, references), you have no legal problem. But what if you have a number of more or less equally qualified applicants? Can you safely choose one who happens to be an older white man over a young Asian woman? If two people rate equally, you can, in theory, choose either one without legal risk. However, if you consistently avoid equally qualified minority applicants, you are guilty of discrimination. (See "Step 2: Advertise the Property," page 24, for a discussion of how to avoid discrimination when looking for tenants.)

You may be eager to rent your property in a hurry. Or, like many landlords, you may be faced with anxious, sometimes desperate people who need a place to live immediately. Some people tell terrific hard-luck stories as to why normal credit and reference-checking rules should be ignored in their case and why they should be allowed to move right in. Don't believe any of it. People who have planned so poorly that they will literally have to sleep in the street if they don't rent your place that day are likely to come up with similar emergencies when it comes time to pay the rent.

⚠ Don't be rushed into a temporary tenancy. Never, never let anyone stay in your property on a temporary basis. Even if you haven't signed a rental agreement or accepted rent, you give the legally protected status of a tenant by giving a person a key or allowing him or her to move in as much as a toothbrush. Then, if the person won't leave voluntarily, you will have to file a lawsuit to evict him or her.

KEEP GOOD RECORDS

A crucial use of any tenant-screening system is to document how and why you chose a particular tenant. Assuming you selected a highly qualified tenant, you want your records to back you up to protect yourself against any charges of illegal discrimination. A good way to do this is to maintain organized files of applications, credit reports and other materials and notes on prospective tenants for at least one year after you rent a particular unit. If your decision not to rent to an applicant is based on oral information provided by a former landlord or employer, make a brief note of your conversation and include it in your file. You can put your notes in the space provided at the bottom of our Rental Application form.

Example: March 15, 199X at 11:35 A.M. Called Kate Steiner's former landlord, Larry Lewis, at 555-1313. Lewis said that Steiner was occasionally one to two weeks late with her rent and kept a cat in her apartment, contrary to the rental agreement.

A final piece of recordkeeping advice: Make sure you update your records after a tenant moves in. You always want to know the tenant's phone number and where he or she works and banks. (You can get this latter information from the monthly rent check if the tenant pays by personal check.) If a tenant leaves owing you money above the security deposit amount, you may be able to collect that money from his or her wages or bank account, if you first sue and receive a court judgment.

Step 6: Provide Disclosures If Required By Law

➡ Skip this step unless your property is either: (1) located within one mile of a former military base or (2) was built before 1979, has 10 or more units and contains asbestos.

Before any tenant signs a lease or rental agreement, he or she must be advised if either of the following applies:

Property is located near former military base. If your property is within a mile of a "former ordnance location"—an abandoned or closed military base in which ammunition or military explosives were used—you must notify all prospective tenants in writing. (CC § 1940.7.) It is not necessary to warn prospective tenants of the existence of current ordnance locations, such as presently-existing army or navy bases.

Use the Disclosures By Property Owner(s) form and check the first box. Then include details in the spaces provided.

Example: "Between 1942 and 1945, the United States Army used the nearby area bounded by 6th and 7th Streets and 1st and 3rd Avenues in the City of Stockton as a reserve training area. Unexploded rifle ammunition and other ordnance have been found there."

If you have the slightest idea your property is within a mile of a former military base or training area, check it out. You might start by asking the reference librarian at a nearby public library or by writing a letter to the local Congressional representative. If you have a particular location in mind, you can also check with the County Recorder, who will show you how to trace the ownership all the way back to the turn of the century for any indication the property was at one time owned or leased by the federal government.

Asbestos. Owners of apartment buildings that have ten or more units and were constructed before 1979 must notify tenants and employees who work in the building if the building contains "asbestos-containing construction materials." The written notice must be given to each employee and tenant *individually*. Failure to notify can result in a fine of up to $1,000, imprisonment of up to one year, or both. (Health & Safety Code §§ 25915 through 25924.)

Use the Disclosures By Property Owner(s) form and check the second box. Provide details in the blanks. Make sure you give a separate copy of the notice to each tenant (as well as to each employee who works in the building). Have each person sign at the bottom of a separate form, and keep the signed original.

Step 7: Cash Rent and Security Deposit Checks

If the new tenant's first rent or deposit check bounces, you might have to undertake time-consuming and expensive legal proceedings to evict a tenant who's paid you nothing.

To avoid this, never sign a rental agreement, let a tenant move furniture into your property or give out a key until:

- you have the tenant's cash, or a certified check or money order for the first month's rent and security deposit, or
- you cash a tenant's check at the bank.

If the tenant's first month's rent is pro-rated for less than half a month's rent, you should request a more substantial amount up front. (See "Other Ways To Handle the Initial Rent Payment," page 12, for different ways to do

DISCLOSURES BY PROPERTY OWNER(S)

The owner(s) of property located at <u>1234 State Avenue, Apartment 5, Los Angeles, California</u>

make(s) the following disclosure(s) to prospective tenant(s) and/or employee(s):

☒ **Location near former military base.** State law requires property owners to disclose to all prospective tenants, before they sign any rental agreement or lease, if the property they are seeking to rent is within one mile of a former ordnance area (military base) as defined by California Civil Code Section 1940.7.
Details regarding the former military base near the property listed above are as follows:
<u>Between 1942-1945, the U.S. Army used the nearby area bounded by 6th and 7th Streets and 1st and 3rd Avenues in the City of Los Angeles as a reserve training area. Unexploded rifle ammunition has been found there.</u>

❑ **Asbestos.** State law requires property owners who own apartment buildings that have ten or more units and were constructed before 1979 to disclose to all prospective tenants, before they sign any rental agreement or lease, and to all employees who work in the building, if the building contains "asbestos-containing construction materials." The written notice must be given to each employee and tenant individually. (Health & Safety Code Sections 25915-25924.)
Information regarding asbestos in the property listed above is as follows:

_____
_____
_____
_____

<u>*Daryl White*</u>   <u>9/19/9X</u>
Owner's Signature   Date

I have read and received a copy of the above Disclosures By Property Owner(s).

_____   _____
Signature   Date

this.) The reason for this is simple. A tenant might impress you in person and look good on an application, but yet be unable to come up with all the rent when due.

Example: Craig moves in on March 21 and pays a security deposit and $300 pro-rated rent for the last ten days of the month. He hopes to find a couple of roommates by the time the regular $900 monthly rent comes due on April 1. If he doesn't come up with the full rent, it will take up to a month to evict him. Craig's landlord will be out a month's rent plus eviction costs. Craig's security deposit may be used to pay for any damage and mess he leaves behind, as well as unpaid rent. Needless to say, Craig's landlord may end up losing hundreds—if not thousands—of dollars under this arrangement.

PREPARE, SIGN AND DISTRIBUTE THE LEASE OR RENTAL AGREEMENT

Here's how to prepare a final lease or rental agreement using the rough draft you filled in. (Instructions for preparing the draft are in "Fill in a Draft Lease or Rental Agreement," beginning on page 7.)

HOW TO PREPARE ATTACHMENT PAGES

Although we have tried to leave adequate blank space on the forms, it's possible that you may run out of room. If you need to add anything to your lease or rental agreement, take the following steps:

Step 1. At the first place you will run out of room, begin your entry and then write "Continued on Attachment 1." Similarly, if there is another place where you'll run out of room, add as much material as you can and then write "Continued on Attachment 2," and so on. Use a separate Attachment each time you need more space.

Step 2. Use the Attachment form provided in this kit or make your own, using a sheet of blank white paper. At the top of the form, fill in the proper number—that is, "Attachment 1" for the first attachment, and so on.

Step 3. Begin each attachment by filling in the number of the clause you're continuing or adding. Then check "a continuation of" if you're continuing a clause, or "an addition to" if you're adding a clause.

Step 4. Type or print the additional information on the Attachment.

Step 5. Both you and each tenant should sign the page at the end of the added material.

Step 6. Staple the Attachment page to the lease or rental agreement.

Prepare the Final Document

Look over your draft lease or rental agreement, making sure that any agreements between you and the tenant have been incorporated. Make sure you have completed Clause 1 (see instructions on page 8).

Take the time to neatly print or type the information on the lease or rental agreement form. If you handwrite the information, make sure you print legibly. You'll then need to:

- sign and date the document
- have the tenant sign and date the document, and
- give a copy of the document to the tenant.

Date and Sign the Document

Be sure your tenant reviews the lease or rental agreement before signing and is clear about all your terms and rules and regulations.

If you changed any clauses, you and each tenant must place your initials next to each such clause. You and each tenant should also sign any Attachment pages. Make sure any Attachment pages, including tenant rules and regulations, are stapled or clipped to the document.

> ⚠️ **Major changes in the lease or rental agreement provisions:** Sometimes a landlord will simply want to add material to a lease or rental agreement (for example, rules having to do with use of a storage room or instructions for how to take care of the yard). To make extensive changes, it will be best to retype or word process our forms, adding your material. But please realize that since leases and rental agreements are heavily regulated by law, it will be your responsibility to be sure your changes are legal. To do this, consult *The Landlord's Law Book, Volume 1: Rights and Responsibilities,* by David Brown & Ralph Warner (Nolo Press) or have your work reviewed by an experienced landlords' lawyer. If you need more room to continue or add a clause, follow the step-by-step instructions below.

In the spaces provided at the end of the document:

- sign as the landlord
- fill in your address, and
- have each tenant sign. There is room for up to three tenants to sign. If there are less than three tenants, cross out the extra signature lines. If there are four or more tenants, have additional tenants sign at the bottom of the form or on the back.

Give Tenants a Copy of the Document

As the landlord, you should keep the original lease or rental agreement. Give the tenants a photocopy of the signed form.

Keep the original lease or rental agreement in a safe place. You may need the document if you need to evict the tenants, or other problems arise with the terms of the tenancy.

Modifying a Signed Lease or Rental Agreement

All amendments to your lease or rental agreement must be in writing to be legally binding.

If you want to change any clauses in a month-to-month rental agreement, there is no legal requirement that you get the tenant's consent (although it's always a good idea to do so). You can simply send the tenant a written 30-day notice of the change, unless a local rent control ordinance requires more notice or prohibits the change you want to make. (The mechanics of sending a 30-day notice to change the terms of a rental agreement are beyond the scope of this kit. See *The Landlord's Law Book, Volume 1: Rights and Responsibilities*, by David Brown & Ralph Warner (Nolo Press).)

If you wish to make mutually agreed-upon changes to a written rental agreement or lease after it is signed, there are two good ways to accomplish it. The first is to agree to substitute a whole new agreement for the old one. The second is to add the new provision as an amendment to the original agreement. An amendment need not have any special form, as long as it clearly refers to the agreement it's changing and is signed by the same people who signed the original agreement. We have included an Amendment to Lease or Rental Agreement form in this kit for your convenience. You can also type or handwrite an amendment; see the sample below.

> **Special rules for rent increases:** You can't increase the rent during the term of a lease. Any rent increases to month-to-month leases require a minimum of 30 days' written notice. In addition, rent control laws may restrict rent increases.

SAMPLE AMENDMENT TO LEASE

The written lease for rental of the premises at 123 Flower Lane, San Diego, California, entered into by Olivia Matthew ("Landlord") and Steve and Sally Phillips ("Tenants") on March 18, 199X is amended as follows:

1. Beginning on June 1, 199X, Tenants shall rent a one-car garage, adjacent to the main premises, from Landlord for the sum of $75 per month.

2. Tenants may keep one German Shepherd dog on the premises. The dog shall be kept on a leash in the yard unless Tenants are present. Tenants shall clean up all animal waste from the yard on a daily basis. Tenants agree to repair any damages to the yard or premises caused by their dog, at Tenants' expense.

Date: May 20, 199X   *Olivia Matthew*
                                  Olivia Matthew, Landlord

Date: May 20, 199X   *Steve Phillips*
                                  Steve Phillips, Tenant

Date: May 20, 199X   *Sally Phillips*
                                  Sally Phillips, Tenant

GET THE TENANTS MOVED IN

Legal disputes between you and your tenants can largely be avoided if—right from the very beginning—you are all clear about your legal rights and responsibilities. A well-drafted lease or rental agreement, signed by all adult occupants, is key to starting a tenancy right. But there's more to getting new tenants moved in. You should also:

- inspect the property and fill in a Landlord/Tenant Checklist
- take pictures of the unit, if you feel it's appropriate, and
- consider preparing a move-in letter highlighting important terms of the tenancy.

Fill In Landlord/Tenant Checklist

It is essential for you and your tenants to check the place over for damage and obvious wear and tear. The easiest way is to fill in a Landlord/Tenant Checklist form provided in this kit.

The Landlord/Tenant Checklist inventories the condition of the rental property. It is an excellent device to protect both you and your tenant when the tenant moves out and wants the security deposit returned. Without some record as to the condition of the unit, you and the tenant are all too likely to get into arguments about things like whether the kitchen linoleum was already stained or the bedroom mirror was cracked when the tenant moved in.

If possible, you and your tenants should fill out the checklist together. If you can't arrange this, complete the form and then give it to the tenant to review. The tenant should make any changes and return it to you.

The first page of the checklist covers the general condition of each room. The second page covers the condition of any furnishings provided, ranging from living room furniture to bathroom shower curtains.

If your rental property has rooms or furnishings not listed on the form, note this under "Other" or "Other Areas," or cross out something that you don't have and write in the furnishings you do have. If you are renting out a large house or apartment or providing many furnishings, you may want to attach a separate sheet.

If your rental unit does not have a particular item listed, such as a dishwasher or kitchen broiler pan, put "N/A" (not applicable) in the "Condition on Arrival" column.

Mark "OK" in the space next to items that are in satisfactory condition.

Make a note—as specific as possible—on items that are not working or are in bad condition. For example, don't note just "needs fixing" if a bathroom sink is clogged; it's as easy to write "clogged drain," so later the tenant can't claim to have told you about the leaky faucet.

The last two columns—*Condition on Departure* and *Estimated Cost of Repair or Replacement*—are for use when the tenant moves out. There you can list information to make deductions from the security deposit for items that need to be repaired, cleaned or replaced.

After you and the tenants agree on all of the particulars, you and each tenant should sign and date the form on both sides as well as any attachments. Keep the original for yourself and attach a copy to the tenant's lease or rental agreement.

Be sure the tenant checks the box on the bottom of the first page of the checklist stating that the smoke detector—required for new occupancies by state law—was tested in his or her presence and shown to be in working order. This section on the checklist also requires the tenant to test the smoke detector monthly and to replace the battery when necessary. By signing this, the tenant has a greater chance of remembering to take care of this important safety measure. You'll also limit your liability if the smoke detector fails and results in fire damage or injury.

Make sure you keep the checklist up-to-date if you repair, replace, add or remove items or furnishings after the tenant moves in. Both you and the tenant should initial and date any changes.

Taking Pictures of the Property

Taking photos or videotapes of the unit before the tenant moves in is another excellent way to avoid disputes over a tenant's responsibility for damage and dirt. When the tenant leaves, you'll be able to compare "before" and "after" pictures.

It's best to take "before" photographs with a Polaroid or other camera that develops pictures automatically; the tenant can then date and sign or initial the pictures on the spot. If possible, you should repeat this process with "after" pictures, to be signed or initialed by the tenant as part of your established move-out procedure.

Consider Sending New Tenants a Move-In Letter

A move-in letter should dovetail with the lease or rental agreement, but cover day-to-day issues, such as how and where to report maintenance problems. A move-in letter can be changed from time to time as necessary. A sample is shown below; you can tailor the letter to meet your particular needs.

SAMPLE MOVE-IN LETTER

October 1, 199X

Dear Mr. O'Hara:

We hope you will enjoy living in the apartment located at 463 Main Street. Our intention is to provide you with a clean, undamaged, pleasant place to live. This letter is to explain what you can expect from us and what we'll be looking for from you.

1. **Rental Agreement:** Your signed copy is attached. Please let us know if you have any questions. A few things we'd like to highlight here:

   - There is no grace period for the payment of rent (see Clause 6 for details, including late charges). Also, we don't accept post-dated checks.

   - If you want someone to move in as a roommate, please contact us. If your rental unit is big enough, we will arrange for the new person to fill out a rental application and, if it's approved, for all of you to sign a new rental agreement.

   - Your security deposit may be applied by us to costs of cleaning, damages or unpaid rent after you move out. You may not apply any part of the deposit, during your tenancy, toward your rent in the last month of your tenancy. (See Clause 8 of your rental agreement.)

   - *(for a month-to-month rental tenancy:)* To terminate your month-to-month tenancy, you must give us at least 30 days' written notice. You may also terminate the tenancy, or change its terms, on 30 days' written notice.

   - *(for a fixed term lease:)* You occupy the premises under a fixed-term lease. You are responsible for all rent payments through the lease term, even if you move out before the lease expires. During the lease term, your rent cannot be increased, nor can other terms of your tenancy be changed.

2. **Landlord/Tenant Checklist:** We couldn't schedule a time to meet with you for a walk-through of your apartment to check the condition of all walls, drapes, carpets, appliances, etc. We've gone through the apartment and listed all of these on the enclosed Landlord/Tenant Checklist. Please read this over carefully and make any changes as you see fit. Then sign and return the form to us right away. When you move out, we will ask you to check each item against its original condition as indicated on the checklist.

3. **Maintenance/Repair Problems:** You have a right to expect repairs to be made promptly. To help us accomplish this, please use one of the enclosed Maintenance/Repair Request forms to report any problems in your apartment or the building or grounds, such as a broken garbage disposal. Except in an emergency, all requests for repairs should be made on this form during normal business hours. In case of emergency, call us at 555-1234.

4. **Telephone Number Changes:** Please notify us if your home or work phone number changes, so we can reach you promptly in case of an emergency.

Please let us know if you have any questions.

Sincerely,

Tony Giuliano
Lori Giuliano

Tony and Lori Giuliano, Landlords

APPENDIX 1: RENT CONTROL CHART

The following chart provides summaries of the specifics of each city's rent control ordinance. For more detail and specifics, and any recent changes, you should obtain a copy of the appropriate ordinance from the address listed after "Administration."

Berkeley

Ordinance Adoption Date	6/3/80; latest amendment 11/90 (ballot measure).
Exceptions	Units constructed after 6/3/80, owner-occupied single-family residences and duplexes. [Sec. 5.]
Administration	Elected nine-member Rent Stabilization Board, 2125 Milvia Street, Berkeley, CA 94704, 510-644-6128.
Registration	Required, or landlord can't raise rents. Stiff penalties for noncooperation. [Secs. 8, 11.f.4, 11.g.]
Rent Formula	Annual general adjustments by Board after investigation and hearings. [Secs. 10, 11.] In 1991, Board allowed property owners to increase what was the base rent in 1980 by 45%, as to those who owned the property as of 12/31/79. In 1992 and 1993, further increases of $26 and $20, respectively, were allowed per rental unit.
Individual Adjustments	Landlord may petition for further increase based on increased taxes or unavoidable increases in utility or maintenance costs, and on costs of capital improvements necessary to bring property up to minimum legal requirements. Increase not allowed based on increased debt service cost due to recent purchase. (If tenant agrees to join in landlord's request, a "fast track" petition method, under which a decision will be made within 30 days and without a formal hearing, may be used.) Tenant may apply for rent reduction based on poor maintenance. [Sec. 12.]
Rent-Increase Notice Requirement	None in addition to state law.
Vacancy Decontrol	No increase allowed upon vacancy. [Ordinance Sec. 6.q allows for decontrol only if rental unit vacancy rate exceeds 5% and both Board and City Council agree; this is a virtual impossibility.]
Eviction	Landlord must show just cause to evict. For other restrictions, see *Landlord's Law Book, Volume 2: Evictions*.
Penalties	Violation of ordinance is misdemeanor punishable by maximums of $500 fine and 90 days imprisonment (first offense) and $3,000 fine and one year imprisonment (second offense). [Sec. 19.] Tenant may sue in court for excess rent collected plus up to $750. [Sec. 15.a]
Other Features	Landlord must place security deposits in interest-bearing savings and loan account which is insured by the Federal Savings and Loan Insurance Corporation, or landlord must pay 10% annual interest. Landlord must credit interest against rents each December, as well as when tenant vacates. [Sec. 7, Regulation Secs. 701, 702.]

Beverly Hills

Ordinance Adoption Date	(Beverly Hills Municipal Code, Chapter 5, Ordinance No. 79-O-1731) 4/27/79; latest amendment 12/9/91.
Exceptions	Units constructed after 10/20/78, units that rented for more than $600 on 5/31/78, single-family residences, rented condominium units. [Sec. 4-5.102.]
Administration	Appointed seven-member Rent Adjustments Board 455 N. Rexford, Beverly Hills, CA 90210, 310-285-1031.
Registration	Not required.
Rent Formula	Except for specific "surcharges" which must be justified and the rent-increase notice (see below), rents may not be increased in any 12-month period by more than 8% (10% where rents were over

$600 in 1979) or a percentage based on the "Urban All Items Consumer Price Index" for Los Angeles, whichever is less. (The CPI-based figure is calculated by adding the monthly CPI figures for the most recently-published 12-month period, subtracting from that a second CPI sum based on the 12-month period before that, and dividing the difference by the lesser of the two sums.) To this permitted increase, the landlord may add a "capital expenditure surcharge" so as to additionally increase the rent by up to 4% more (calculated by amortizing capital improvement costs), a "utility expense surcharge" based on owner-paid utility cost increases in excess of the allowed annual percentage increase, and a 10% surcharge for each adult tenant occupying the unit over and above any maximum number of adult occupants specified in the lease. The landlord may also pass through the amortized cost of any legally-required improvements. [Secs. 4-5.302-4-5.307.]

Individual Adjustments Tenant who contests validity of any capital improvement surcharge or utility surcharge over and above the annual increase percentage may petition Board to request non-allowance of the surcharge. Landlord seeking increases above annual percentage increase and allowed surcharges may apply to Board for higher "hardship" increase. (Ordinance is silent on factors to be considered, but does not preclude hardship increase based on high debt service costs due to recent purchase.) [Sec. 4-5.402.]

Rent-Increase Notice Requirement Landlord must post in the lobby, hallway, or other "public" location on the property a notice stating the name, address, and telephone number of the owner or authorized agent, and must give each tenant a copy of the notice; failure to comply with this requirement precludes increase of rents. Rent-increase notice must state the basis justifying any rent increase above the basic rent formula, and must advise the tenant that records and documentation verifying it will be made available for inspection by the tenant or the tenant's representative. [Sec. 4-5.309.] The justification should break down the increase into portions allowed under annual adjustment and individual surcharges.

Vacancy Decontrol Landlord may charge any rent after a tenant vacates voluntarily, but not when landlord terminates tenancy. Once the property is re-rented, it is subject to rent control based on the higher rent. [Sec. 4-5.310.]

Eviction Landlord must show just cause to evict. For other restrictions, see *Landlord's Law Book, Volume 2: Evictions*.

Penalties Violation of ordinance is a misdemeanor punishable by maximums of $500 fine and six months imprisonment. [Sec. 4-5.706.] Tenant may sue in court for three times any rent in excess of legal rent collected ($500 minimum), plus attorney fees. [Sec. 4-5.705.]

Campbell

Ordinance Adoption Date 1983 (Campbell Municipal Code, Chapter 6.09); latest amendment 1990.

Exceptions Single-family residences and duplexes. [Sec. 6.09.030(I).]

Administration Campbell Rent Mediation program, 1245 S. Winchester Blvd. Suite 200, San Jose, CA 95128, l408-243-8565.

Registration Not required.

Rent Formula No fixed formula; rent increases must be "reasonable." [Sec. 6.09.150.]

Individual Adjustments Tenants in 25% of the units (but at least three units) affected by an increase can contest it by filing a petition within 37 days, or lose the right to object to the increase. Disputes raised by tenant petition are first subject to "conciliation," then mediation. If those fail, either party may file written request for arbitration by city "Fact Finding Committee." Committee determines whether increase is "reasonable" by considering costs of capital improvements, repairs, maintenance, and debt service, and past history of rent increases. However, the Committee's determination is not binding. [Secs. 6.09.050-6.09.150.]

Rent-Increase Notice Requirement	On written request by a tenant, an apartment landlord must disclose in writing to that person the apartment numbers of all tenants receiving rent increases that same month. [Sec. 6.09.040.]
Vacancy Decontrol	No restriction on raises after vacancy.
Eviction Features	Ordinance does not require showing of just cause to evict, so 3-day and 30-day notice requirements and unlawful detainer procedures are governed solely by state law.
Note	Because this ordinance does not provide for binding arbitration of any rent-increase dispute, it is not truly a rent control ordinance. Compliance with any decision appears to be voluntary only.

Cotati

Ordinance Adoption Date	(Cotati Municipal Code, Chapter 19.19), 9/23/80 (ballot initiative); latest amendment 3/10/87.
Exceptions	Units constructed after 9/23/80 (board has authority to remove exemption), owner-occupied single-family residences, duplexes, and triplexes. [Sec. 19.12.020.D.]
Administration	Appointed five-member Rent Appeals Board, 201 W. Sierra, Cotati, CA 94931, 707-792-4600.
Registration	Required, or landlord can't raise rents, and tenants can seek Board permission to withhold current rents (but may have to pay all or part of withheld rent to landlord after registration). [Sec. 19.12.030.O.][1]
Rent Formula	9/23/80 freeze at 6/1/79 levels, plus annual "general adjustments" by Board after investigation and hearings. [Sec. 19.12.050.] Annual general adjustment is to be adequate to cover operating cost increases and to permit net operating income to increase at 66% of the rate of increase in the CPI (Consumer Price Index [all items] for urban consumers, San Francisco-Oakland). [Regulation Secs. 3000-3002.]
Individual Adjustments	Within 30 days after Board determines annual general adjustment, landlord may petition for further increase based on increased taxes or unavoidable increases in utility or maintenance costs, and on costs of capital improvements necessary to bring property up to minimum legal requirements. Increase not allowed based on increased debt service cost due to recent purchase. Tenant may apply for rent reduction based on poor maintenance. [Secs. 19.12.060, 19.12.070, Reg. Secs. 4001-4052.]
Rent-Increase Notice Requirements	None in addition to state law.
Vacancy Decontrol	None. [Ordinance Sec. 19.12.030.P allows Board to decontrol only housing whose rental unit vacancy rate exceeds 5%; this is highly unlikely.]
Eviction	Landlord must show just cause to evict. For other restrictions, see *Landlord's Law Book, Volume 2: Evictions*.
Penalties	Tenant may sue in court for three times any excess rent collected ($500 minimum) plus attorney fees, or tenant may simply credit any excess payments against future rent payments. [Sec. 19.12.110.]
Other Features	Landlord must place security deposits in interest-bearing insured savings and loan account and credit interest to tenant when she vacates. [Sec. 19.12.150]

---

[1] Since the Board must first approve rent-withholding following a hearing, this provision may still be valid despite *Floystrup v. Berkeley Rent Stabilization Board,* 219 Cal. App. 3d 1309 (1990).

East Palo Alto

Ordinance Adoption Date	11/23/83; latest amendment 4/88.
Exceptions	Units constructed after 11/23/83, units owned by landlords owning four or fewer units in city. [Sec. 5.]
Administration	Appointed seven-member Rent Stabilization Board, 2415 University Ave., East Palo Alto, CA 94303, 415-853-3100.
Registration	Required, or landlord can't raise rents, and tenants can apply to Board for permission to withhold current rents (but may have to pay all or part of withheld rent to landlord after registration). [Secs. 8, 11.E.4, 15.A.1.][2]
Rent Formula	11/23/83 freeze at 4/1/83 levels, plus annual adjustments by Board after investigation and hearings. [Secs. 10, 11.]
Individual Adjustments	Landlord may apply for further increase based on increased taxes or unavoidable increases in utility or maintenance costs, and on costs of capital improvements necessary to bring property up to minimum legal requirements. Increase not allowed based on increased debt service due to recent purchase. Tenant may apply for rent reduction based on poor maintenance. [Sec. 12.]
Rent-Increase Notice Requirements	Notices increasing rent by more than that allowed under annual across-the-board adjustment must state that it is subject to appeal by tenant petition to Board, and must list Board address and telephone number. [Sec.12.E.]
Vacancy Decontrol	No increases allowed upon vacancy.
Eviction	Landlord must show just cause to evict. For other restrictions, see *Landlord's Law Book, Volume 2: Evictions*.
Penalties	Violation of ordinance is misdemeanor punishable by maximums of $500 fine and 90 days imprisonment (first offense) and $3,000 fine and one year imprisonment (second offense). [Sec. 19.] Tenant may sue landlord in court for excess rent unlawfully collected plus up to $500. [Sec. 15.A.4.]
Other Features	Landlord must place security deposits in interest-bearing account at an insured bank or savings and loan and credit interest against rents each December, as well as when tenant vacates. [Sec. 7.]

Hayward

Ordinance Adoption Date	9/13/83; latest amendment 3/16/93.
Exceptions	Units first occupied after 7/1/79, units owned by landlord owning four or fewer rental units in the city. [Sec. 2(l).]
Administration	Administered by city-manager-appointed employees of Rent Review Office, 25151 Clawiter Rd., Hayward, CA 94545-2731, 510-293-5540.
Registration	Not required.
Rent Formula	Annual rent increases limited in any 12-month period to 5%, plus increased utility costs if documented as specified. A landlord who has not increased the rent during a previous 12-month period may "bank" the increase by raising it 10% the next period. [Sec. 3(c),(d).]
Individual Adjustments	The tenant can contest an increase of over 5% by first contacting the person specified in the notice (see notice requirements, below) for an explanation of the increase. Tenant then must file petition with the Rent Review Office before the increase takes effect (30 days) or lose the right to object to it. Disputes raised in tenant petition are heard by a mediator; if mediation fails, arbitration is mandatory and binding on both parties. Landlord may be allowed to pass on increased utility and maintenance costs and "amortize" (spread out) capital expenditures. [Sec. 5.]

---

[2] Since the Board must first approve rent-withholding following a hearing, this provision may still be valid despite *Floystrup v. Berkeley Rent Stabilization Board,* 219 Cal. App. 3d 1309 (1990).

Rent-Increase Notice Requirements	Landlord must give tenant a copy of ordinance at the beginning of the tenancy, and a document which gives the unit's rent history and lists improvements to the unit. [Sec. 4(a).] Failure to comply may be grounds for denial of an otherwise-proper rent increase. Rent-increase notices must be accompanied by a blank tenant petition form, and by a second notice which either states that the increase is allowed under the 5%-increase limitation or which gives specific reasons for an increase above 5%. The notice must also include the name, address, and telephone number of the landlord or other person able to explain the increase. [Sec. 4(b).]
Vacancy Decontrol	Rent controls are permanently removed from each unit after a voluntary vacancy (that is, without any legal action by or notices from the landlord, even for cause), followed by the expenditure of $200 or more on improvements by the landlord, and city certification of compliance with city Housing Code.[Sec. 8.]
Eviction	Landlord must show just cause to evict, even where rent control removed by vacancy decontrol, above. For other restrictions, see *Landlord's Law Book, Volume 2: Evictions*.
Penalties	Failure to provide required information to tenant is an infraction (petty offense) punishable on first, second, or third offense within 12-month period by fines of up to $100, $200 and $500, respectively. Fourth offense within 12 months is misdemeanor punishable by maximums of $1,000 fine and six months imprisonment. [Sec. 20.b.] Tenant may sue in court for excess rent collected, treble that amount or $500 (whichever is greater), and attorney fees. [Sec. 20.a.]
Other Features	Ordinance requires landlords holding security deposits longer than a year to pay annual interest at a rate determined by the Rent Review officer by November 1st of each year, based on local passbook savings rates. Interest must be credited against the tenant's rent on his anniversary date and when deposit refunded at end of tenancy. There is, however, no requirement for separate account. Violation can subject landlord to liability for three times the amount of unpaid interest owed. [Sec. 13.]

Los Angeles

Ordinance Adoption Date	(Los Angeles Municipal Code, Chapter XV), 4/21/79; latest amendment 2/19/91.
Exceptions	Units constructed (or substantially renovated with at least $10,000 in improvements) after 10/1/78, "luxury" units (defined as 0,1,2,3, or 4+-bedroom units renting for at least $302, $420, $588, $756, or $823, respectively, as of 5/31/78), single-family residences, except where three or more houses are located on the same lot. [Sec. 151.02.G,M.]
Administration	Appointed seven-member Rent Adjustment Commission, 400 South Main, 6th Floor, Los Angeles, CA 90013. For information regarding ordinance, call 213-847-7368.
Registration	Required.[3] [Sec. 151.11.B] Tenant may defend any unlawful detainer action on the basis of the landlord's failure to register the property [Sec. 151.09.F].
Rent Formula	Except with permission of Commission or Community Development Department, rents may not be increased by more than a 3%-to-8% percentage based on the "Urban All Items Consumer Price Index" for the Los Angeles/Long Beach/Anaheim/Santa Monica/Santa Ana areas. The figure is published each year by the Community Development Department on or before May 30th, and applies to rent increases to be effective the following July 1st through June 30th of the next year. The actual percentage is calculated by averaging the CPI over the previous 12-month period beginning the September 30th before that, but in any event cannot fall below 3% or exceed 8%. In addition, if the landlord pays for gas or electricity for the unit, she may raise the rent an additional 1% for each such type of utility service. [Secs. 151.06.D, 151.07.A.6.]

---

[3]The ordinance's provision that tenants may withhold rents for non-registration is unconstitutional, unless ordinance allows the landlord a hearing first. See *Floystrup v. Berkeley Rent Stabilization Board,* 219 Cal. App. 3d 1309 (1990).

Individual Adjustments	Landlord may apply to the Rent Adjustment Commission for higher increase to obtain "just and reasonable return." (This does not include "negative cash flow" based on recent purchase, but does include negative "operating expense," not counting landlord's mortgage payment.) [Sec. 151.07.B] Also, landlord may apply to Community Development Department for permission to pass on to the tenant 50% of the cost of capital improvements not directly benefiting the landlord—for example, new roof costs would be considered, but not costs of renovations to manager's units or advertising signs—spread out over five or more years [Sec. 151.07.A].
Rent-Increase Notice Requirements	Landlord must post conspicuously or give tenant a copy of current registration statement showing that the property is registered with Board. [Sec. 151.05.A.] Landlord who applies to Board for a rent higher than maximum is required to provide written justification for the difference. [Sec. 151.05.C.]
Vacancy Decontrol	Landlord may charge any rent after a tenant either vacates voluntarily or is evicted for nonpayment of rent, breach of a rental agreement provision, or to substantially remodel. Controls remain if landlord evicts for any other reason, fails to remodel after evicting for that purpose, or terminates or fails to renew a subsidized-housing lease with the city housing authority. Once a vacated unit is re-rented, it is subject to rent control based on the higher rent. [Sec. 151.06.C.]
Eviction	Landlord must show just cause to evict. For other restrictions, see *Landlord's Law Book, Volume 2: Evictions.*
Penalties	Violation of ordinance, including failing to include proper information in eviction notices, is a misdemeanor punishable by maximums of $500 fine and six months imprisonment. [Sec. 151.10.B.] Tenant may sue in court for three times any rent in excess of legal rent collected, plus attorney fees. [Sec. 151.10.A.]
Other Features	Landlord must pay 5% annual interest rate on deposits held over a year. Interest payments need only be made every five years, and when deposit refunded at end of tenancy. (This part of the ordinance, however, is not being enforced at this time, while a legal challenge proceeds through the appeals courts.)
	Los Angeles also has a Rent Escrow Adjustment Program (REAP) ordinance that applies to all rent-controlled units. Under this ordinance, a tenant whose landlord has received a 30-day notice from local health or building inspectors to correct serious housing code violations may withhold rent and pay it to a city escrow fund, if the landlord has failed to correct the violation within the 30-day period. (See Chapter 11 for details on REAP.)

Los Gatos

Ordinance Adoption Date	(Los Gatos Town Code, Chapter 24), 10/27/80; latest amendment 12/5/83. (Later amendments apply to mobile home parks only.)
Exceptions	Property on lots with two or fewer units, single-family residences, rented condominium units. [Sec. 24.20.015.]
Administration	Los Gatos Rent Mediation program, 1245 S. Winchester Blvd., Suite 200, San Jose, CA 95128, 408-243-8565.
Registration	Not required. (However, a "regulatory fee" to pay for program is added to annual business license fee, when business license is required.)
Rent Formula	Rents may not be increased more than once within 12-month period (except to pass through regulatory fee), and are limited to 5% or 70% of the "Urban All Items Consumer Price Index" for the San Francisco-Oakland area. [Secs. 24.30.010, 24.70.015(3).]
Individual Adjustments	Tenants in 25% of the units affected by an increase greater than the formula above can contest it by filing a petition within 30 days, or will lose the right to object to the increase. Disputes initiated by tenant petition are first attempted to be resolved by "conciliation." If that fails, either party may file a written request for mediation, and, if that fails, binding arbitration. [Secs. 24.40.010-

	24.40.050.] Mediator/arbitrator may consider costs of capital improvements, repairs, maintenance, and debt service, and past history of rent increases. [Regulation Secs. 2.03-2.05.]
Rent-Increase Notice Requirements	Rent-increase notice for increases above 5% (or separate statement served with it) must state, "You have the right to use the Rental Dispute Mediation and Arbitration Hearing Process. For further information contact Los Gatos Rent Mediation Program," giving program's address and telephone number. On written request by a tenant, an apartment landlord must disclose in writing to that person the apartment numbers of all tenants receiving rent increases that same month. [Sec. 24.30.030.]
Vacancy Decontrol	Landlord may charge any rent after a tenant vacates voluntarily or is evicted following 3-day notice for nonpayment of rent or other breach of the rental agreement. Once the property is re-rented, it is subject to rent control based on the higher rent. [Sec. 24.70.015(1).]
Eviction	Ordinance does not require showing of just cause to evict, but tenant has other defenses. For other restrictions, see *Landlord's Law Book, Volume 2: Evictions*.
Other Features	Mediation/arbitration process applies not only to rent increases and evictions, but also to provision of "housing services". [Sec. 24.40.010.] Since ordinance requires that every lease and rental agreement include a provision to agree to binding arbitration [Sec. 24.40.040], a party invoking the process can in effect keep a "housing services" dispute out of the courts—this will make any binding arbitration award final.

Oakland

Ordinance Adoption Date	10/7/80; latest amendment 10/28/86.
Exceptions	Units constructed after 1/1/83, buildings "substantially rehabilitated" at cost of 50% of that of new construction (as determined by Chief Building Inspector) properties with HUD-insured mortgages. [Sec. 2.i].
Administration	Appointed 7-member Residential Rent Arbitration Board, 300 Lakeside Drive, Oakland, CA 94612, 510-238-3721 (to leave message) or call Sentinel Fair Housing, 510-836-2687.
Registration	Not required.
Rent Formula	Rents may not be increased more than 6% in any 12-month period for occupied units, and 12% in any 12-month period for units vacated after the landlord terminated the tenancy. [Sec. 5.]
Individual Adjustments	Tenant can contest an increase in excess of that allowed (but only if his rent is current) by filing a petition with the Board. The petition must be filed within 30 days. Hearing officer may consider costs of capital improvements, repairs, maintenance, and debt service, and past history of rent increases. [Sec. 5.c.,7.]
Rent-Increase Notice Requirements	Landlords are required to notify tenants of the Residential Rent Arbitration Board at outset of the tenancy, in an addendum to the lease or rental agreement. [Sec. 5.d.]
Vacancy Decontrol	Landlord may charge any rent after a tenant vacates voluntarily. Controls remain if tenant vacates "involuntarily," though 12-month rent-increase ceiling increases to 12% from 8%. Once the property is re-rented, it is subject to rent control based on the higher rent. [Sec. 5.b.] Controls may be permanently removed if landlord spends at least 50% of new-construction cost to "substantially rehabilitate" property.
Eviction	Ordinance does not require just cause to evict, but there are other requirements. For other restrictions, see *Landlord's Law Book, Volume 2: Evictions*.
Penalties	Violation of ordinance is infraction (petty offense) punishable on first, second, and third offenses within 12-month period by fines of up to $50, $100, and $250, respectively. A fourth offense within 12 months is a misdemeanor punishable by maximums of a $500 fine and six months imprisonment. [Sec. 9.1.]

Palm Springs

Ordinance Adoption Date	(Palm Springs Municipal Code, Title 4), 9/1/79 (ballot initiative); latest amendment 4/10/90.
Exceptions	Units constructed after 4/1/79, owner-occupied single-family residences, duplexes, triplexes, and four-plexes, units where rent was $450 or more as of 9/1/79. [Secs. 4.02.010, 4.02.030.]
Administration	Appointed five-member Rent Review Commission, 3200 E. Tahquitz Canyon, Palm Springs, CA 92262, 619-778-8465.
Registration	Required, or landlord can't raise rents. [Sec. 4.02.080.]
Rent Formula	Rent as of 9/1/79, plus annual increases not exceeding 75% of the annual "Urban All Items Consumer Price Index" for the Los Angeles/Long Beach/Anaheim metropolitan area. (Step-by-step calculation procedure is set forth in ordinance.) [Secs. 4.02.040, 4.02.050.]
Individual Adjustments	Landlord may petition for further increases based on "hardship." Commission consent for increase is not necessary if tenant agrees in writing, but landlord may not coerce consent under threat of eviction or nonrenewal of lease, and may not include general waiver in lease or rental agreement. [Secs. 4.02.060, 4.02.065.]
Rent-Increase Notice Requirements	Before raising rent, landlord must notify tenant in writing of the base rent charged on 9/1/79, the present rent, and the date of the last previous rent increase. [Sec. 4.02.080(d)(2).] This information can be included on the rent-increase notice.
Vacancy Decontrol	No increases allowed when vacancy occurs.
Eviction	Just cause to evict is not required, but there may be other restrictions. For other restrictions, see *Landlord's Law Book, Volume 2: Evictions*.
Penalties	Tenant may sue in court for any excess rent collected, attorney fees, and a penalty of up to $300. [Sec. 4.02.090.] Tenant may also seek the $300-plus-attorney-fees penalty against landlord who coerces consent to rent increase. [Sec. 4.02.060(c).]

San Francisco

Ordinance Adoption Date	(San Francisco Administrative Code, Chapter 37), 6/79; latest amendment 12/18/92.
Exceptions	Units constructed after 6/79, buildings over 50 years old and "substantially rehabilitated" since 6/79, owner-occupied single-family residences, duplexes, triplexes, and four-plexes. [Sec. 37.2(p).]
Administration	Appointed five-member Residential Rent Stabilization and Arbitration Board, [Sec. 37.4], 25 Van Ness Avenue, Suite 320, San Francisco, CA 94102, 415-554-9550 and 415-554-9551.
Registration	Not required.
Rent Formula	Rents may not be increased by more than 7% in any 12-month period. (Increase allowed each year is 60% of the "Urban All Items Consumer Price Index" for the San Francisco-Oakland Metropolitan Area, but not more than 7%.) The figure is published each year by the Board. [Sec. 37.3.] A landlord who has not increased the rent during a previous 12-month period may accumulate his/her rights to increases and impose them in later years. Landlord may apply to Board for certification of capital improvements the amortized cost of which may also be passed through to the tenant, but such increases are limited to 10% of the base rent each year. [Sec. 37.7.]
Individual Adjustments	Landlord may apply to Board for higher increase based on increased costs, including utility and capital-improvement costs. Hearing officer decides case based on various factors, including operating and maintenance expenses, but not "negative cash flow" based on recent purchase. Hearing officer may also consider rent-increase history and failure to make repairs. Tenant may contest any claimed pass through of utility costs, or request rent reduction based on decrease of services or poor maintenance. Either party may request an "expedited hearing." [Secs. 37.8.]

Rent-Increase Notice Requirements	Landlord must give tenant written itemized breakdown of rent increases—for example, what portion reflects costs of capital improvements—on or before the date of service of the rent-increase notice. [Sec. 37.6(b).]
Vacancy Decontrol	Landlord may charge any rent after a tenant vacates voluntarily or is evicted for good cause. Once the property is re-rented, it is subject to rent control based on the higher rent. [Sec. 37.3(a).]
Eviction	Landlord must show just cause to evict. [Sec. 37.9.] For other restrictions, see *Landlord's Law Book, Volume 2: Evictions*.
Penalties	Violation of ordinance, including wrongful eviction or eviction attempts, is a misdemeanor punishable by maximums of a $2,000 fine and six months imprisonment. [Sec. 37.10.]
Other Features	Landlord must pay 5% annual interest on deposits held over a year, with payments made on tenant's move-in anniversary date each year, and when deposit refunded at end of tenancy. [Administrative Code, Chapter 49.]

San Jose

Ordinance Adoption Date	(San Jose Municipal Code, Title 17, Chapter 17.23) 7/7/79; latest amendment 7/19/91.
Exceptions	Units constructed after 9/7/79, single-family residences, duplexes, and condominium units. [Sec. 17.23.150.]
Administration	Appointed seven-member Advisory Commission on Rents, 4 N. Second St., Suite 600, San Jose, CA 95113-1305, 408-277-5431.
Registration	Required.
Rent Formula	Rents may not be increased more than 8% in any 12-month period, and may not be increased more than once within the 12 months. However, a landlord who has not raised the rent for over 24 months is entitled to a 21% increase. [Secs. 17.23.180, 17.23.210.]
Individual Adjustments	Tenant can contest an increase in excess of that allowed by filing a petition before rent increase takes effect (30 days), or lose the right to object. Disputes initiated by tenant petition are heard by a mediation hearing officer, who may consider costs of capital improvements, repairs, maintenance, and debt service, and past history of rent increases. Either party may appeal mediator's decision and invoke binding arbitration. Tenant can also petition to contest rent based on housing-code violations or decrease in services. [Secs. 17.23.220-17.23.440.]
Rent-Increase Notice Requirement	Where rent increase exceeds 8%, rent-increase notice must advise tenant of her right to utilize the Rental Dispute Mediation and Arbitration Hearing Process, giving the address and telephone number of the city's rent office. The notice must also indicate the time limit within which the tenant may do this. [Sec. 17.23.270.]
Vacancy Decontrol	Landlord may charge any rent after a tenant vacates voluntarily or is evicted following three-day notice for nonpayment of rent or other breach of the rental agreement. Once the property is re-rented, it is subject to rent control based on the higher rent. [Sec. 17.23.190.]
Eviction	Ordinance does not require showing of just cause to evict.
Penalties	Violation of ordinance by charging rent in excess of that allowed following mediation/arbitration, by retaliation against the tenant for asserting his rights, or by attempting to have tenant waive rights under ordinance is a misdemeanor punishable by maximums of a $500 fine and six months imprisonment. [Secs. 17.23.515-17.23.530.] Tenant may sue landlord in court for excess rents charged, plus treble damages or $500 (whichever is greater) [Sec. 17.23.540.]

Santa Monica

Ordinance Adoption Date	(City Charter Article XVIII), 4/10/79 (ballot initiative); latest amendment 9/13/91.
Exceptions	Units constructed after 4/10/79, owner-occupied single-family residences, duplexes, and triplexes, single-family houses not rented on 7/1/84. [Charter Amendment (C.A.) Secs. 1801(c), 1815, Regulation (Reg.) Secs. 2000+, 12000+.]
Administration	Elected five-member Rent Control Board, 1685 Main St., Room 202, Santa Monica, CA 90401, 310-458-8751.
Registration	Required, or landlord can't raise rents. [C.A. Secs. 1803(q), 1805(h).]
Rent Formula	4/10/79 freeze at 4/10/78 levels, plus annual adjustments by Board. [C.A. Secs. 1804, 1805(a),(b), Reg. Secs. 3000+.]
Individual Adjustments	Landlord may apply for further increase based on increased taxes or unavoidable increases in utility or maintenance costs, capital improvements, but not "negative cash flow" due to recent purchase. Tenant may apply for rent reduction based on poor maintenance or decrease in services. [C.A. Sec. 1805(c)-(h), Reg. Secs. 4000+.]
Rent-Increase Notice Requirements	Rent-increase notice must state, "The undersigned [landlord] certifies that this unit and common areas are not subject to any uncorrected citation or notices of violation of any state or local housing, health, or safety laws issued by any government official or agency, and that all registration fees have been paid to date." [Reg. Sec. 3007(f)(3)]. Otherwise, tenant may refuse to pay increase and successfully defend unlawful detainer action based on failure to pay increase.
Vacancy Decontrol	None. [C.A. Sec. 1803(r) allows Board to decontrol any category of property only if the rental unit vacancy rate exceeds 5%; this is a virtual impossibility.] However, under "Threshold Program," landlord may petition for limited increase following voluntary vacancy, if rent is below a certain level, depending on type and location of property.
Eviction	Landlord must show just cause to evict. For other restrictions, see *Landlord's Law Book, Volume 2: Evictions*.
Penalties	Violation of the charter amendment is a misdemeanor punishable by maximums of a $500 fine and six months imprisonment. Tenant may sue landlord in court for violating ordinance in any way, and may recover attorney fees; tenant may recover rents unlawfully charged, plus treble damages and attorney fees. [C.A. Sec. 1809(a)(d).]
Other Features	Landlord must place security deposits in interest-bearing account at insured savings and loan or bank. Landlord need not pay tenant any of the interest, but failure to do so is a "factor" in the city denying an individual landlord's requested rent increase (or granting a tenant's requested rent decrease). Landlord cannot raise security deposit during tenancy, even if rent is raised, unless tenant agrees. [City Charter Article XV111, Chapter 14.]

Thousand Oaks

Ordinance Adoption Date	7/1/80; latest amendment 3/24/87.
Exceptions	Units constructed after 6/30/80, "luxury" units (defined as 0,1,2,3, or 4+-bedroom units renting for at least $400, $500, $600, $750, or $900, respectively, as of 6/30/80), single-family residences, duplexes, triplexes, and four-plexes, except where five or more units are located on the same lot. [Sec. III.L.]
Administration	Appointed five-member Rent Adjustment Commission, 2400 Willow Lane, Thousand Oaks, CA 91361, 805-497-8611, ext. 657.
Registration	Required. [Sec. XIV.]

Rent Formula	Rents may not be increased by more than 7% in any 12-month period. Increase allowed each year is 75% of the "Urban All Items Consumer Price Index" for the greater Los Angeles area, but not less than 3% nor more than 7%. [Secs. III.G,H, VI.]
Individual Adjustments	Landlord may apply to the Rent Adjustment Commission for higher increase based on capital improvement costs, or to obtain "just and reasonable return" (does not include "negative cash flow" based on recent purchase.) [Sec. VII.]
Rent-Increase Notice Requirements	Landlord must prominently post in the apartment complex a listing or map of rental units, showing which are subject to the ordinance and which are not. [Sec. VI.C.]
Vacancy Decontrol	Property that becomes vacant after 5/1/81 due to tenant voluntarily leaving or being evicted for nonpayment of rent is no longer subject to any provision of the ordinance. [Sec. VI.]
Eviction Features	Landlord must show just cause to evict. For other restrictions, see *Landlord's Law Book, Volume 2: Evictions*.
Penalties	Tenant may sue in court for three times any rent in excess of legal rent collected, plus a penalty of up to $500 and attorney's fees. [Sec. IX.]
Other Features	Landlord can exempt property from rent control by offering "freedom leases" with five-year term and yearly increase of no more than 3% where the tenant is over age 65, or three-year term with yearly increase of no more than 75% of the All-Urban Consumers CPI for the greater Los Angeles area, for non-elderly tenants.

West Hollywood

Ordinance Adoption Date	(West Hollywood Municipal Code, Article IV, Chapter 4), 6/27/85 (ballot initiative); latest amendment 8/93.
Exceptions	Units constructed after 7/1/79 ("just-cause" eviction requirements do apply, however). However, all exemptions (except a standard "boarding" exemption) must be applied for in registration document (see below). [Sec. 6406.]
Administration	Appointed five-member Rent Stabilization Commission, 8704 Santa Monica Blvd. (mailing address is 8611 Santa Monica Boulevard), West Hollywood, CA 90069, 310-854-7450.
Registration	Required, or landlord can't raise rents. [Sec. 6407.]
Rent Formula	11/29/84 freeze at 4/30/84 levels, plus annual adjustments by Board of no more than 75% of the "Urban All Items Consumer Price Index" for the greater Los Angeles area. Landlords who pay for tenants' gas and/or electricity may increase an additional 1/2 % for each such utility. [Secs. 6408, 6409.] But total increase can't exceed 10%.
Individual Adjustments	Landlord may apply for further increase based on unavoidable increases in utility or maintenance costs or taxes, and for capital improvement, or on basis of not receiving fair rate of return, if owner owned property as of 4/30/84. Tenant may apply for rent reduction based on poor maintenance. [Sec. 6411.] Also, Board may initiate a hearing on the same basis. [Sec. 6414(k).]
Rent-Increase Notice Requirements	Rent-increase notice must contain statement to the effect that landlord is in compliance with ordinance, including filing and payment of required registration documents and fees. [Sec. 6409.G, Regulation Sec. 40000(f).]
Vacancy Decontrol	When tenant of property other than a single-family dwelling voluntarily vacates or is evicted for cause, landlord may increase rent by additional 10%; however, no more than one such increase is permitted within any 60-month period. When tenant of single-family dwelling (where there's one unit per parcel only) voluntarily vacates or is evicted for cause (other than for occupancy by owner or relative), landlord can raise rent to any level; once the single-family dwelling is re-rented, it is subject to rent control at the new higher rent. In other units, rent remains controlled after vacancy,

	and landlord must disclose new maximum rent to new tenant, or else later request for increase may be disallowed. In either case, landlord must file "vacancy increase certificate" with city and show she has repainted and cleaned carpets and drapes within previous six months, that all appliances are in working order, and that the premises are free from health or safety violations. Certificate must be filed within 30 days after re-occupancy, or landlord cannot raise rent under this provision. [Sec. 6410.]
Eviction	Landlord must show just cause to evict. For other restrictions, see *Landlord's Law Book, Volume 2: Evictions*.
Penalties	Violation of ordinance is misdemeanor punishable by maximums of $1,000 fine and six months imprisonment. [Sec. 6414.E.] Tenant may sue landlord in court for three times any rents collected or demanded in excess of legal rents, plus attorney fees. [Sec. 6414.C.]
Other Features	Landlord must pay or credit interest on security deposits against rents, in January or February of each year, as well as when tenant vacates. [Sec. 6408.B.]

Westlake Village

This small city (population 10,000) has a rent control ordinance that applies to apartment complexes of five units or more (as well as to mobile-home parks, whose specialized laws are not covered in this book.) Because the city's only apartment complex of this size has undergone conversion to condominiums, there is therefore now no property (other than mobile home parks) to which the ordinance applies, so we don't explain the ordinance here.

APPENDIX 2:
LEASE & RENTAL AGREEMENT FORMS

Form	Copies Provided
Rental Application	2
Month-to-Month Residential Rental Agreement	2
Fixed-Term Residential Lease	2
Attachment to Lease or Rental Agreement	2
Attachment: Agreement Regarding Use of Waterbed	1
Landlord/Tenant Checklist	2
Disclosures By Property Owner(s)	1
Receipt	1
Amendment to Lease or Rental Agreement	2
Maintenance/Repair Request	2
Security Deposit Itemization	1

RENTAL APPLICATION

Separate application required from each applicant age 18 or older.

[this section to be completed by landlord]

Address of Property to be Rented: _____

Amounts Due Prior to Occupancy:

First month's rent $ _____

Security deposit (may not be used toward last month's rent) $ _____

Other (specify): $ _____

Total $ _____

Applicant

Full Name—include all names you use(d): _____

Home Phone: ( ) _____ Work Phone: ( ) _____

Social Security Number: _____ Driver's License Number/State: _____

Vehicle Make: _____ Model: _____ Color: _____ Year: _____

License Plate Number/State: _____

Additional Occupants

List everyone who will live with you:

Full Name	Relationship to Applicant	Co-signer on lease? (yes/no)

Rental History

Current Address: _____

Dates Lived at Address: _____ Reason for Leaving: _____

Landlord/Manager: _____ Landlord/Manager's Phone: ( ) _____

Previous Address: _____

Dates Lived at Address: _____ Reason for Leaving: _____

Landlord/Manager: _____ Landlord/Manager's Phone: ( ) _____

Previous Address: _____

Dates Lived at Address: _____ Reason for Leaving: _____

Landlord/Manager: _____ Landlord/Manager's Phone: ( ) _____

Employment History

Name and Address of Current Employer: _____

Phone: ( ) _____

Name of Supervisor: _____ Supervisor's Phone: ( ) _____

How Long with This Employer: _____ Position or Title: _____

Name and Address of Previous Employer: _____

Phone: ( ) _____

Name of Supervisor: _____ Supervisor's Phone: ( ) _____

How Long with This Employer: _____ Position or Title: _____

Income Information

1. Your gross monthly employment income (before deductions) $ _____
2. Average monthly amounts of other income (specify sources): $ _____
3. Total monthly household income (sum of two items above) $ _____

Credit and Financial Information

Bank/Financial Accounts	Account Number	Bank/Institution	Branch
Savings Account:			
Checking Account:			
Money Market or Similar Account:			

Credit Accounts & Loans	Type of Account (Auto loan, Visa, etc.)	Account Number	Name of Creditor	Amount Owed	Monthly Payment
Major Credit Card:					
Major Credit Card:					
Loan (car, student loan, etc.):					
Other Major Obligation:					

Miscellaneous

Describe how many and what type of pets you want to have in the rental property:

_____

Describe water-filled furniture you want to have in the rental property: _____

Do you smoke? ❏ yes ❏ no

Have you ever: Filed for bankruptcy? ❏ yes ❏ no   Been sued? ❏ yes ❏ no   Been evicted? ❏ yes ❏ no

Explain any "yes" listed above: _____

_____

References and Emergency Contact

Personal Reference: _____ Relationship: _____

Address: _____

_____ Phone: (___) _____

Personal Reference: _____ Relationship: _____

Address: _____

_____ Phone: (___) _____

Contact in Emergency: _____ Relationship: _____

Address: _____

_____ Phone: (___) _____

I certify that all the information given above is true and correct and understand that my lease or rental agreement may be terminated if I have made any misrepresentation in this application. I authorize verification of any of the information and references provided in this application. In addition to all sums due prior to occupancy, I agree to pay a *nonrefundable* fee of $_____, which shall be used to obtain a report on my credit from a credit reporting agency.

Date _____ Signed _____

NOTES (Landlord/Manager):

Rental Application

RENTAL APPLICATION

Separate application required from each applicant age 18 or older.

[*this section to be completed by landlord*]

Address of Property to be Rented: _____

Amounts Due Prior to Occupancy:

First month's rent $ _____

Security deposit (may not be used toward last month's rent) $ _____

Other (specify): $ _____

Total $ _____

Applicant

Full Name—include all names you use(d): _____

Home Phone: ( ) _____ Work Phone: ( ) _____

Social Security Number: _____ Driver's License Number/State: _____

Vehicle Make: _____ Model: _____ Color: _____ Year: _____

License Plate Number/State: _____

Additional Occupants

List everyone who will live with you:

Full Name	Relationship to Applicant	Co-signer on lease? (yes/no)

Rental History

Current Address: _____

Dates Lived at Address: _____ Reason for Leaving: _____

Landlord/Manager: _____ Landlord/Manager's Phone: ( ) _____

Previous Address: _____

Dates Lived at Address: _____ Reason for Leaving: _____

Landlord/Manager: _____ Landlord/Manager's Phone: ( ) _____

Previous Address: _____

Dates Lived at Address: _____ Reason for Leaving: _____

Landlord/Manager: _____ Landlord/Manager's Phone: ( ) _____

Employment History

Name and Address of Current Employer: _____

Phone: ( ) _____

Name of Supervisor: _____ Supervisor's Phone: ( ) _____

How Long with This Employer: _____ Position or Title: _____

Name and Address of Previous Employer: _____

Phone: ( ) _____

Name of Supervisor: _____ Supervisor's Phone: ( ) _____

How Long with This Employer: _____ Position or Title: _____

Income Information

1. Your gross monthly employment income (before deductions) $ _____
2. Average monthly amounts of other income (specify sources): $ _____
3. Total monthly household income (sum of two items above) $ _____

Credit and Financial Information

Bank/Financial Accounts	Account Number	Bank/Institution	Branch
Savings Account:			
Checking Account:			
Money Market or Similar Account:			

Credit Accounts & Loans	Type of Account (Auto loan, Visa, etc.)	Account Number	Name of Creditor	Amount Owed	Monthly Payment
Major Credit Card:					
Major Credit Card:					
Loan (car, student loan, etc.):					
Other Major Obligation:					

Miscellaneous

Describe how many and what type of pets you want to have in the rental property:
_____

Describe water-filled furniture you want to have in the rental property: _____

Do you smoke? ❑ yes ❑ no

Have you ever: Filed for bankruptcy? ❑ yes ❑ no   Been sued? ❑ yes ❑ no   Been evicted? ❑ yes ❑ no

Explain any "yes" listed above: _____
_____

References and Emergency Contact

Personal Reference: _____   Relationship: _____
Address: _____
_____   Phone: (_____) _____

Personal Reference: _____   Relationship: _____
Address: _____
_____   Phone: (_____) _____

Contact in Emergency: _____   Relationship: _____
Address: _____
_____   Phone: (_____) _____

I certify that all the information given above is true and correct and understand that my lease or rental agreement may be terminated if I have made any misrepresentation in this application. I authorize verification of any of the information and references provided in this application. In addition to all sums due prior to occupancy, I agree to pay a *nonrefundable* fee of $_____, which shall be used to obtain a report on my credit from a credit reporting agency.

Date _____   Signed _____

NOTES (Landlord/Manager):

Rental Application   2

MONTH-TO-MONTH RESIDENTIAL RENTAL AGREEMENT

1. **Identification of Landlord and Tenants.** This Agreement is made and entered into on _____, 19____, between _____ ("Tenants") and _____ ("Landlord"). Each Tenant is jointly and severally liable for the payment of rent and performance of all other terms of this Agreement.

2. **Identification of Premises and Occupants.** Subject to the terms and conditions set forth in this Agreement, Landlord rents to Tenants, and Tenants rent from Landlord, for residential purposes only, the premises located at _____, California ("the premises"). The premises shall be occupied by the undersigned Tenants and the following minor children: _____.

3. **Limits on Use and Occupancy.** The premises are to be used only as a private residence for Tenants and any minors listed in Clause 2 of this Agreement, and for no other purpose without Landlord's prior written consent. Occupancy by guests for more than ten days in any six-month period is prohibited without Landlord's written consent and shall be considered a breach of this Agreement.

4. **Defining the Term of the Tenancy.** The rental shall begin on _____, 19____, and shall continue on a month-to-month basis. This tenancy may be terminated by Landlord or Tenants and may be modified by Landlord, by giving 30-days' written notice to the other (subject to any local rent control ordinances that may apply).

5. **Amount and Schedule for the Payment of Rent.** Tenants shall pay to Landlord a monthly rent of $_____, payable in advance on the _____ day of each month, except when that day falls on a weekend or legal holiday, in which case rent is due on the next business day. Rent shall be paid to _____ at _____, or at such other place as Landlord shall designate from time to time.
   - ❏ a. The form of payment shall be _____.
   - ❏ b. On signing this Agreement, Tenants shall pay to Landlord for the period of _____, 19____, through _____, 19____, the sum of $_____ as rent, payable in advance.

6. **Late Charges.** Tenants shall pay Landlord a late charge if Tenants fail to pay the rent in full within _____ days after the date it is due. The late charge shall be $_____, plus $_____ for each additional day that the rent continues to be unpaid. The total late charge for any one month shall not exceed $_____. Landlord does not waive the right to insist on payment of the rent in full on the date it is due.

7. **Returned Check and Other Bank Charges.** In the event any check offered by Tenants to Landlord in payment of rent or any other amount due under this Agreement is returned for lack of sufficient funds, a "stop payment" or any other reason, Tenants shall pay Landlord a returned check charge in the amount of $_____.

8. **Amount and Payment of Deposits.** On signing this Agreement, Tenants shall pay to Landlord the sum of $_____ as a security deposit. Tenants may not, without Landlord's prior written consent, apply this security deposit to the last month's rent or to any other sum due under this Agreement. Within three weeks after Tenants have vacated the premises, Landlord shall furnish Tenants with an itemized written statement of the reasons for, and the dollar amount of, any of the security deposit retained by the Landlord, along with a check for any deposit balance. Under Section 1950.5 of the California Civil Code, Landlord may withhold only that portion of Tenants' security deposit necessary to: (1) remedy any default by Tenants in the payment of rent; (2) repair damages to the premises exclusive of ordinary wear and tear; and (3) clean the premises if necessary.

Landlord shall pay Tenants interest on all security deposits as follows:

❑ a. Under local law, no interest payments are required.

❑ b. Local law requires that interest be paid or credited, which shall occur as follows:

_____
_____

9. **Utilities.** Tenants shall be responsible for payment of all utility charges, except for the following, which shall be paid by Landlord:

_____

❑ Tenants' gas or electric meter serves area(s) outside of their premises and there are not separate gas and electric meters for Tenants' unit and the area(s) outside their unit. Tenants and Landlord agree as follows:

_____
_____

10. **Prohibition of Assignment and Subletting.** Tenants shall not sublet any part of the premises or assign this Agreement without the prior written consent of Landlord.

11. **Condition of the Premises.** Tenants agree to: (1) keep the premises clean and sanitary and in good repair and, upon termination of the tenancy, to return the premises to Landlord in a condition identical to that which existed when Tenants took occupancy, except for ordinary wear and tear; (2) immediately notify Landlord of any defects or dangerous conditions in and about the premises of which they become aware; and (3) reimburse Landlord, on demand by Landlord, for the cost of any repairs to the premises damaged by Tenants or their guests or invitees through misuse or neglect.

    Tenants acknowledge that they have examined the premises, including appliances, fixtures, carpets, drapes and paint, and have found them to be in good, safe and clean condition and repair, except as noted here:

_____
_____
_____
_____

12. **Possession of the Premises.** If, after signing this Agreement, Tenants fail to take possession of the premises, they shall still be responsible for paying rent and complying with all other terms of this Agreement. In the event Landlord is unable to deliver possession of the premises to Tenants for any reason not within Landlord's control, including, but not limited to, failure of prior occupants to vacate or partial or complete destruction of the premises, Tenants shall have the right to terminate this Agreement. In such event, Landlord's liability to Tenants shall be limited to the return of all sums previously paid by Tenants to Landlord.

13. **Pets.** No animal, bird or other pet shall be kept on the premises without Landlord's prior written consent, except properly trained dogs needed by blind, deaf or physically disabled persons and:

❑ a. None.

❑ b. _____, under the following conditions:

_____

14. **Landlord's Access for Inspection and Emergency.** Landlord or Landlord's agents may enter the premises in the event of an emergency to make repairs or improvements, supply agreed services and show the premises to prospective buyers or tenants. Except in cases of emergency, Tenants' abandonment of the premises or court order, Landlord shall give Tenants reasonable notice of intent to enter and shall enter only during regular business hours of Monday through Friday from 9:00 a.m. to 6:00 p.m. and Saturday from 10:00 a.m. to 1:00 p.m.

15. Extended Absences By Tenants. Tenants agree to notify Landlord in the event that they will be away from the premises for _____ consecutive days or more. During such absence, Landlord may enter the premises at times reasonably necessary to maintain the property and inspect for damage and needed repairs.

16. Prohibitions Against Violating Laws and Causing Disturbances. Tenants shall be entitled to quiet enjoyment of the premises. Tenants and their guests or invitees shall not use the premises or adjacent areas in such a way as to: (1) violate any law or ordinance, including laws prohibiting the use, possession or sale of illegal drugs; (2) commit waste or nuisance; or (3) annoy, disturb, inconvenience or interfere with the quiet enjoyment and peace and quiet of any other tenant or nearby resident.

17. Repairs and Alterations

   a. Tenants shall not, without Landlord's prior written consent, alter, re-key or install any locks to the premises or install or alter any burglar alarm system. Tenants shall provide Landlord with a key or keys capable of unlocking all such re-keyed or new locks as well as instructions on how to disarm any altered or new burglar alarm system.

   b. Except as provided by law or as authorized by the prior written consent of Landlord, Tenants shall not make any repairs or alterations to the premises.

   ❑ Landlord and Tenants agree to the following:

   _____
   _____
   _____

18. Damage to the Premises. In the event the premises are partially or totally damaged or destroyed by fire or other cause, the following shall apply:

   a. If the premises are totally damaged and destroyed, Landlord shall have the option to: (1) repair such damage and restore the premises, with this Agreement continuing in full force and effect, except that Tenants' rent shall be abated while repairs are being made; or (2) give written notice to Tenants terminating this Agreement at any time within thirty (30) days after such damage, and specifying the termination date; in the event that Landlord gives such notice, this Agreement shall expire and all of Tenants' rights pursuant to this Agreement shall cease.

   b. Landlord shall have the option to determine that the premises are only partially damaged by fire or other cause. In that event, Landlord shall attempt to repair such damage and restore the premises within thirty (30) days after such damage. If only part of the premises cannot be used, Tenants must pay rent only for the usable part, to be determined solely by Landlord. If Landlord is unable to complete repairs within thirty (30) days, this Agreement shall expire and all of Tenants' rights pursuant to this Agreement shall terminate at the option of either party.

   c. In the event that Tenants, or their guests or invitees, in any way caused or contributed to the damage of the premises, Landlord shall have the right to terminate this Agreement at any time, and Tenants shall be responsible for all losses, including, but not limited to, damage and repair costs as well as loss of rental income.

   d. Landlord shall not be required to repair or replace any property brought onto the premises by Tenants.

19. Tenants' Financial Responsibility and Renters' Insurance. Tenants agree to accept financial responsibility for any loss or damage to personal property belonging to Tenants and their guests and invitees caused by theft, fire or any other cause. Landlord assumes no liability for any such loss. Landlord recommends that Tenants obtain a renter's insurance policy from a recognized insurance firm to cover Tenants' liability, personal property damage and damage to the premises.

20. Waterbeds. No waterbed or other item of water-filled furniture shall be kept on the premises without Landlord's written consent.

   ❑ Landlord grants Tenants permission to keep water-filled furniture on the premises. Attachment _____: Agreement Regarding Use of Waterbed is attached to and incorporated into this Agreement by reference.

21. Tenant Rules and Regulations

   ❑ Tenants acknowledge receipt of, and have read a copy of, tenant rules and regulations, which are labeled Attachment _____ and attached to and incorporated into this Agreement by reference.

22. **Payment of Attorney Fees in a Lawsuit.** In any action or legal proceeding to enforce any part of this Agreement, the prevailing party ❑ shall not/ ❑ shall recover reasonable attorney fees and court costs.

23. **Authority to Receive Legal Papers.** Any person managing the premises, the owner and anyone designated by the owner are authorized to accept service of process and receive other notices and demands, which may be delivered to:

❑ a. The manager, at the following address: _____

_____

❑ b. The owner, at the following address: _____

_____

❑ c. The following: _____

_____

24. Additional Provisions

❑ a. None

❑ b. Additional provisions are as follows:
_____
_____
_____

25. **Entire Agreement.** This document constitutes the entire Agreement between the parties, and no promises or representations, other than those contained here and those implied by law, have been made by Landlord or Tenants. Any modifications to this Agreement must be in writing signed by Landlord and Tenants. The failure of Tenants or their guests or invitees to comply with any term of this Agreement is grounds for termination of the tenancy, with appropriate notice to tenants and procedures as required by law.

_____ _____
Landlord/Manager   Date

_____
Landlord/Manager's Street Address, City, State & Zip

_____ _____
Tenant   Date

_____ _____
Tenant   Date

_____ _____
Tenant   Date

MONTH-TO-MONTH RESIDENTIAL RENTAL AGREEMENT

1. **Identification of Landlord and Tenants.** This Agreement is made and entered into on _____, 19_____, between _____ ("Tenants") and _____ ("Landlord"). Each Tenant is jointly and severally liable for the payment of rent and performance of all other terms of this Agreement.

2. **Identification of Premises and Occupants.** Subject to the terms and conditions set forth in this Agreement, Landlord rents to Tenants, and Tenants rent from Landlord, for residential purposes only, the premises located at _____, California ("the premises"). The premises shall be occupied by the undersigned Tenants and the following minor children: _____.

3. **Limits on Use and Occupancy.** The premises are to be used only as a private residence for Tenants and any minors listed in Clause 2 of this Agreement, and for no other purpose without Landlord's prior written consent. Occupancy by guests for more than ten days in any six-month period is prohibited without Landlord's written consent and shall be considered a breach of this Agreement.

4. **Defining the Term of the Tenancy.** The rental shall begin on _____, 19_____, and shall continue on a month-to-month basis. This tenancy may be terminated by Landlord or Tenants and may be modified by Landlord, by giving 30-days' written notice to the other (subject to any local rent control ordinances that may apply).

5. **Amount and Schedule for the Payment of Rent.** Tenants shall pay to Landlord a monthly rent of $_____, payable in advance on the _____ day of each month, except when that day falls on a weekend or legal holiday, in which case rent is due on the next business day. Rent shall be paid to _____ at _____, or at such other place as Landlord shall designate from time to time.

   ❑ a. The form of payment shall be _____.

   ❑ b. On signing this Agreement, Tenants shall pay to Landlord for the period of _____, 19_____, through _____, 19_____, the sum of $_____ as rent, payable in advance.

6. **Late Charges.** Tenants shall pay Landlord a late charge if Tenants fail to pay the rent in full within _____ days after the date it is due. The late charge shall be $_____; plus $_____ for each additional day that the rent continues to be unpaid. The total late charge for any one month shall not exceed $_____. Landlord does not waive the right to insist on payment of the rent in full on the date it is due.

7. **Returned Check and Other Bank Charges.** In the event any check offered by Tenants to Landlord in payment of rent or any other amount due under this Agreement is returned for lack of sufficient funds, a "stop payment" or any other reason, Tenants shall pay Landlord a returned check charge in the amount of $_____.

8. **Amount and Payment of Deposits.** On signing this Agreement, Tenants shall pay to Landlord the sum of $_____ as a security deposit. Tenants may not, without Landlord's prior written consent, apply this security deposit to the last month's rent or to any other sum due under this Agreement. Within three weeks after Tenants have vacated the premises, Landlord shall furnish Tenants with an itemized written statement of the reasons for, and the dollar amount of, any of the security deposit retained by the Landlord, along with a check for any deposit balance. Under Section 1950.5 of the California Civil Code, Landlord may withhold only that portion of Tenants' security deposit necessary to: (1) remedy any default by Tenants in the payment of rent; (2) repair damages to the premises exclusive of ordinary wear and tear; and (3) clean the premises if necessary.

Landlord shall pay Tenants interest on all security deposits as follows:

❑ a. Under local law, no interest payments are required.

❑ b. Local law requires that interest be paid or credited, which shall occur as follows:
_____
_____

9. **Utilities.** Tenants shall be responsible for payment of all utility charges, except for the following, which shall be paid by Landlord:
_____
_____

❑ Tenants' gas or electric meter serves area(s) outside of their premises and there are not separate gas and electric meters for Tenants' unit and the area(s) outside their unit. Tenants and Landlord agree as follows:
_____
_____

10. **Prohibition of Assignment and Subletting.** Tenants shall not sublet any part of the premises or assign this Agreement without the prior written consent of Landlord.

11. **Condition of the Premises.** Tenants agree to: (1) keep the premises clean and sanitary and in good repair and, upon termination of the tenancy, to return the premises to Landlord in a condition identical to that which existed when Tenants took occupancy, except for ordinary wear and tear; (2) immediately notify Landlord of any defects or dangerous conditions in and about the premises of which they become aware; and (3) reimburse Landlord, on demand by Landlord, for the cost of any repairs to the premises damaged by Tenants or their guests or invitees through misuse or neglect.

    Tenants acknowledge that they have examined the premises, including appliances, fixtures, carpets, drapes and paint, and have found them to be in good, safe and clean condition and repair, except as noted here:
_____
_____
_____
_____

12. **Possession of the Premises.** If, after signing this Agreement, Tenants fail to take possession of the premises, they shall still be responsible for paying rent and complying with all other terms of this Agreement. In the event Landlord is unable to deliver possession of the premises to Tenants for any reason not within Landlord's control, including, but not limited to, failure of prior occupants to vacate or partial or complete destruction of the premises, Tenants shall have the right to terminate this Agreement. In such event, Landlord's liability to Tenants shall be limited to the return of all sums previously paid by Tenants to Landlord.

13. **Pets.** No animal, bird or other pet shall be kept on the premises without Landlord's prior written consent, except properly trained dogs needed by blind, deaf or physically disabled persons and:

❑ a. None.

❑ b. _____, under the following conditions:
_____

14. **Landlord's Access for Inspection and Emergency.** Landlord or Landlord's agents may enter the premises in the event of an emergency to make repairs or improvements, supply agreed services and show the premises to prospective buyers or tenants. Except in cases of emergency, Tenants' abandonment of the premises or court order, Landlord shall give Tenants reasonable notice of intent to enter and shall enter only during regular business hours of Monday through Friday from 9:00 a.m. to 6:00 p.m. and Saturday from 10:00 a.m. to 1:00 p.m.

15. **Extended Absences By Tenants.** Tenants agree to notify Landlord in the event that they will be away from the premises for _____ consecutive days or more. During such absence, Landlord may enter the premises at times reasonably necessary to maintain the property and inspect for damage and needed repairs.

16. **Prohibitions Against Violating Laws and Causing Disturbances.** Tenants shall be entitled to quiet enjoyment of the premises. Tenants and their guests or invitees shall not use the premises or adjacent areas in such a way as to: (1) violate any law or ordinance, including laws prohibiting the use, possession or sale of illegal drugs; (2) commit waste or nuisance; or (3) annoy, disturb, inconvenience or interfere with the quiet enjoyment and peace and quiet of any other tenant or nearby resident.

17. **Repairs and Alterations**
    a. Tenants shall not, without Landlord's prior written consent, alter, re-key or install any locks to the premises or install or alter any burglar alarm system. Tenants shall provide Landlord with a key or keys capable of unlocking all such re-keyed or new locks as well as instructions on how to disarm any altered or new burglar alarm system.
    b. Except as provided by law or as authorized by the prior written consent of Landlord, Tenants shall not make any repairs or alterations to the premises.
    ❑ Landlord and Tenants agree to the following:
    _____
    _____
    _____

18. **Damage to the Premises.** In the event the premises are partially or totally damaged or destroyed by fire or other cause, the following shall apply:
    a. If the premises are totally damaged and destroyed, Landlord shall have the option to: (1) repair such damage and restore the premises, with this Agreement continuing in full force and effect, except that Tenants' rent shall be abated while repairs are being made; or (2) give written notice to Tenants terminating this Agreement at any time within thirty (30) days after such damage, and specifying the termination date; in the event that Landlord gives such notice, this Agreement shall expire and all of Tenants' rights pursuant to this Agreement shall cease.
    b. Landlord shall have the option to determine that the premises are only partially damaged by fire or other cause. In that event, Landlord shall attempt to repair such damage and restore the premises within thirty (30) days after such damage. If only part of the premises cannot be used, Tenants must pay rent only for the usable part, to be determined solely by Landlord. If Landlord is unable to complete repairs within thirty (30) days, this Agreement shall expire and all of Tenants' rights pursuant to this Agreement shall terminate at the option of either party.
    c. In the event that Tenants, or their guests or invitees, in any way caused or contributed to the damage of the premises, Landlord shall have the right to terminate this Agreement at any time, and Tenants shall be responsible for all losses, including, but not limited to, damage and repair costs as well as loss of rental income.
    d. Landlord shall not be required to repair or replace any property brought onto the premises by Tenants.

19. **Tenants' Financial Responsibility and Renters' Insurance.** Tenants agree to accept financial responsibility for any loss or damage to personal property belonging to Tenants and their guests and invitees caused by theft, fire or any other cause. Landlord assumes no liability for any such loss. Landlord recommends that Tenants obtain a renter's insurance policy from a recognized insurance firm to cover Tenants' liability, personal property damage and damage to the premises.

20. **Waterbeds.** No waterbed or other item of water-filled furniture shall be kept on the premises without Landlord's written consent.
    ❑ Landlord grants Tenants permission to keep water-filled furniture on the premises. Attachment _____: Agreement Regarding Use of Waterbed is attached to and incorporated into this Agreement by reference.

21. **Tenant Rules and Regulations**
    ❑ Tenants acknowledge receipt of, and have read a copy of, tenant rules and regulations, which are labeled Attachment _____ and attached to and incorporated into this Agreement by reference.

22. Payment of Attorney Fees in a Lawsuit. In any action or legal proceeding to enforce any part of this Agreement, the prevailing party ❑ shall not/ ❑ shall recover reasonable attorney fees and court costs.

23. Authority to Receive Legal Papers. Any person managing the premises, the owner and anyone designated by the owner are authorized to accept service of process and receive other notices and demands, which may be delivered to:

❑ a. The manager, at the following address: _____

_____

❑ b. The owner, at the following address: _____

_____

❑ c. The following: _____

_____

24. Additional Provisions

❑ a. None

❑ b. Additional provisions are as follows:

_____
_____
_____

25. Entire Agreement. This document constitutes the entire Agreement between the parties, and no promises or representations, other than those contained here and those implied by law, have been made by Landlord or Tenants. Any modifications to this Agreement must be in writing signed by Landlord and Tenants. The failure of Tenants or their guests or invitees to comply with any term of this Agreement is grounds for termination of the tenancy, with appropriate notice to tenants and procedures as required by law.

_____   _____
Landlord/Manager   Date

_____
Landlord/Manager's Street Address, City, State & Zip

_____   _____
Tenant   Date

_____   _____
Tenant   Date

_____   _____
Tenant   Date

FIXED-TERM RESIDENTIAL LEASE

1. **Identification of Landlord and Tenants.** This Agreement is made and entered into on _____, 19_____, between _____ ("Tenants") and _____ ("Landlord"). Each Tenant is jointly and severally liable for the payment of rent and performance of all other terms of this Agreement.

2. **Identification of Premises and Occupants.** Subject to the terms and conditions set forth in this Agreement, Landlord rents to Tenants, and Tenants rent from Landlord, for residential purposes only, the premises located at _____, California ("the premises"). The premises shall be occupied by the undersigned Tenants and the following minor children: _____.

3. **Limits on Use and Occupancy.** The premises are to be used only as a private residence for Tenants and any minors listed in Clause 2 of this Agreement, and for no other purpose without Landlord's prior written consent. Occupancy by guests for more than ten days in any six-month period is prohibited without Landlord's written consent and shall be considered a breach of this Agreement.

4. **Defining the Term of the Tenancy.** The term of the rental shall begin on _____, 19_____, and shall expire on _____, 19_____. Should Tenants vacate before expiration of the term, Tenants shall be liable for the balance of the rent for the remainder of the term, less any rent Landlord collects or could have collected from a replacement tenant by reasonably attempting to re-rent. Tenants who vacate before expiration of the term are also responsible for Landlord's costs of advertising for a replacement tenant.

5. **Amount and Schedule for the Payment of Rent.** Tenants shall pay to Landlord a monthly rent of $_____, payable in advance on the _____ day of each month, except when that day falls on a weekend or legal holiday, in which case rent is due on the next business day. Rent shall be paid to _____ at _____, or at such other place as Landlord shall designate from time to time.
   - ☐ a. The form of payment shall be _____.
   - ☐ b. On signing this Agreement, Tenants shall pay to Landlord for the period of _____, 19_____, through _____, 19_____, the sum of $_____ as rent, payable in advance.

6. **Late Charges.** Tenants shall pay Landlord a late charge if Tenants fail to pay the rent in full within _____ days after the date it is due. The late charge shall be $_____, plus $_____ for each additional day that the rent continues to be unpaid. The total late charge for any one month shall not exceed $_____. Landlord does not waive the right to insist on payment of the rent in full on the date it is due.

7. **Returned Check and Other Bank Charges.** In the event any check offered by Tenants to Landlord in payment of rent or any other amount due under this Agreement is returned for lack of sufficient funds, a "stop payment" or any other reason, Tenants shall pay Landlord a returned check charge in the amount of $_____.

8. **Amount and Payment of Deposits.** On signing this Agreement, Tenants shall pay to Landlord the sum of $_____ as a security deposit. Tenants may not, without Landlord's prior written consent, apply this security deposit to the last month's rent or to any other sum due under this Agreement. Within three weeks after Tenants have vacated the premises, Landlord shall furnish Tenants with an itemized written statement of the reasons for, and the dollar amount of, any of the security deposit retained by the Landlord, along with a check for any deposit balance. Under Section 1950.5 of the California Civil Code, Landlord may withhold only that portion of Tenants' security deposit necessary to: (1) remedy any default by Tenants in the payment of rent; (2) repair damages to the premises exclusive of ordinary wear and tear; and (3) clean the premises if necessary.

Landlord shall pay Tenants interest on all security deposits as follows:

❑ a. Under local law, no interest payments are required.

❑ b. Local law requires that interest be paid or credited, which shall occur as follows:

_____
_____

9. Utilities. Tenants shall be responsible for payment of all utility charges, except for the following, which shall be paid by Landlord:

_____

❑ Tenants' gas or electric meter serves area(s) outside of their premises and there are not separate gas and electric meters for Tenants' unit and the area(s) outside their unit. Tenants and Landlord agree as follows:

_____
_____

10. Prohibition of Assignment and Subletting. Tenants shall not sublet any part of the premises or assign this Agreement without the prior written consent of Landlord.

11. Condition of the Premises. Tenants agree to: (1) keep the premises clean and sanitary and in good repair and, upon termination of the tenancy, to return the premises to Landlord in a condition identical to that which existed when Tenants took occupancy, except for ordinary wear and tear; (2) immediately notify Landlord of any defects or dangerous conditions in and about the premises of which they become aware; and (3) reimburse Landlord, on demand by Landlord, for the cost of any repairs to the premises damaged by Tenants or their guests or invitees through misuse or neglect.

Tenants acknowledge that they have examined the premises, including appliances, fixtures, carpets, drapes and paint, and have found them to be in good, safe and clean condition and repair, except as noted here:

_____
_____
_____
_____

12. Possession of the Premises. If, after signing this Agreement, Tenants fail to take possession of the premises, they shall still be responsible for paying rent and complying with all other terms of this Agreement. In the event Landlord is unable to deliver possession of the premises to Tenants for any reason not within Landlord's control, including, but not limited to, failure of prior occupants to vacate or partial or complete destruction of the premises, Tenants shall have the right to terminate this Agreement. In such event, Landlord's liability to Tenants shall be limited to the return of all sums previously paid by Tenants to Landlord.

13. Pets. No animal, bird or other pet shall be kept on the premises without Landlord's prior written consent, except properly trained dogs needed by blind, deaf or physically disabled persons and:

❑ a. None.

❑ b. _____, under the following conditions:

_____

14. Landlord's Access for Inspection and Emergency. Landlord or Landlord's agents may enter the premises in the event of an emergency to make repairs or improvements, supply agreed services and show the premises to prospective buyers or tenants. Except in cases of emergency, Tenants' abandonment of the premises or court order, Landlord shall give Tenants reasonable notice of intent to enter and shall enter only during regular business hours of Monday through Friday from 9:00 a.m. to 6:00 p.m. and Saturday from 10:00 a.m. to 1:00 p.m.

15. Extended Absences By Tenants. Tenants agree to notify Landlord in the event that they will be away from the premises for _____ consecutive days or more. During such absence, Landlord may enter the premises at times reasonably necessary to maintain the property and inspect for damage and needed repairs.

16. Prohibitions Against Violating Laws and Causing Disturbances. Tenants shall be entitled to quiet enjoyment of the premises. Tenants and their guests or invitees shall not use the premises or adjacent areas in such a way as to: (1) violate any law or ordinance, including laws prohibiting the use, possession or sale of illegal drugs; (2) commit waste or nuisance; or (3) annoy, disturb, inconvenience or interfere with the quiet enjoyment and peace and quiet of any other tenant or nearby resident.

17. Repairs and Alterations

a. Tenants shall not, without Landlord's prior written consent, alter, re-key or install any locks to the premises or install or alter any burglar alarm system. Tenants shall provide Landlord with a key or keys capable of unlocking all such re-keyed or new locks as well as instructions on how to disarm any altered or new burglar alarm system.

b. Except as provided by law or as authorized by the prior written consent of Landlord, Tenants shall not make any repairs or alterations to the premises.

❑ Landlord and Tenants agree to the following:

_____
_____
_____

18. Damage to the Premises. In the event the premises are partially or totally damaged or destroyed by fire or other cause, the following shall apply:

a. If the premises are totally damaged and destroyed, Landlord shall have the option to: (1) repair such damage and restore the premises, with this Agreement continuing in full force and effect, except that Tenants' rent shall be abated while repairs are being made; or (2) give written notice to Tenants terminating this Agreement at any time within thirty (30) days after such damage, and specifying the termination date; in the event that Landlord gives such notice, this Agreement shall expire and all of Tenants' rights pursuant to this Agreement shall cease.

b. Landlord shall have the option to determine that the premises are only partially damaged by fire or other cause. In that event, Landlord shall attempt to repair such damage and restore the premises within thirty (30) days after such damage. If only part of the premises cannot be used, Tenants must pay rent only for the usable part, to be determined solely by Landlord. If Landlord is unable to complete repairs within thirty (30) days, this Agreement shall expire and all of Tenants' rights pursuant to this Agreement shall terminate at the option of either party.

c. In the event that Tenants, or their guests or invitees, in any way caused or contributed to the damage of the premises, Landlord shall have the right to terminate this Agreement at any time, and Tenants shall be responsible for all losses, including, but not limited to, damage and repair costs as well as loss of rental income.

d. Landlord shall not be required to repair or replace any property brought onto the premises by Tenants.

19. Tenants' Financial Responsibility and Renters' Insurance. Tenants agree to accept financial responsibility for any loss or damage to personal property belonging to Tenants and their guests and invitees caused by theft, fire or any other cause. Landlord assumes no liability for any such loss. Landlord recommends that Tenants obtain a renter's insurance policy from a recognized insurance firm to cover Tenants' liability, personal property damage and damage to the premises.

20. Waterbeds. No waterbed or other item of water-filled furniture shall be kept on the premises without Landlord's written consent.

❑ Landlord grants Tenants permission to keep water-filled furniture on the premises. Attachment _____: Agreement Regarding Use of Waterbed is attached to and incorporated into this Agreement by reference.

21. Tenant Rules and Regulations

❏ Tenants acknowledge receipt of, and have read a copy of, tenant rules and regulations, which are labeled Attachment _____ and attached to and incorporated into this Agreement by reference.

22. Payment of Attorney Fees in a Lawsuit.
In any action or legal proceeding to enforce any part of this Agreement, the prevailing party ❏ shall not/ ❏ shall recover reasonable attorney fees and court costs.

23. Authority to Receive Legal Papers.
Any person managing the premises, the owner and anyone designated by the owner are authorized to accept service of process and receive other notices and demands, which may be delivered to:

❏ a. The manager, at the following address: _____

❏ b. The owner, at the following address: _____

❏ c. The following: _____

24. Additional Provisions

❏ a. None

❏ b. Additional provisions are as follows:

_____
_____
_____

25. Entire Agreement.
This document constitutes the entire Agreement between the parties, and no promises or representations, other than those contained here and those implied by law, have been made by Landlord or Tenants. Any modifications to this Agreement must be in writing signed by Landlord and Tenants. The failure of Tenants or their guests or invitees to comply with any term of this Agreement is grounds for termination of the tenancy, with appropriate notice to tenants and procedures as required by law.

_____   _____
Landlord/Manager   Date

_____
Landlord/Manager's Street Address, City, State & Zip

_____   _____
Tenant   Date

_____   _____
Tenant   Date

_____   _____
Tenant   Date

FIXED-TERM RESIDENTIAL LEASE

1. **Identification of Landlord and Tenants.** This Agreement is made and entered into on _____, 19_____, between _____ ("Tenants") and _____ ("Landlord"). Each Tenant is jointly and severally liable for the payment of rent and performance of all other terms of this Agreement.

2. **Identification of Premises and Occupants.** Subject to the terms and conditions set forth in this Agreement, Landlord rents to Tenants, and Tenants rent from Landlord, for residential purposes only, the premises located at _____, California ("the premises"). The premises shall be occupied by the undersigned Tenants and the following minor children: _____.

3. **Limits on Use and Occupancy.** The premises are to be used only as a private residence for Tenants and any minors listed in Clause 2 of this Agreement, and for no other purpose without Landlord's prior written consent. Occupancy by guests for more than ten days in any six-month period is prohibited without Landlord's written consent and shall be considered a breach of this Agreement.

4. **Defining the Term of the Tenancy.** The term of the rental shall begin on _____, 19_____, and shall expire on _____, 19_____. Should Tenants vacate before expiration of the term, Tenants shall be liable for the balance of the rent for the remainder of the term, less any rent Landlord collects or could have collected from a replacement tenant by reasonably attempting to re-rent. Tenants who vacate before expiration of the term are also responsible for Landlord's costs of advertising for a replacement tenant.

5. **Amount and Schedule for the Payment of Rent.** Tenants shall pay to Landlord a monthly rent of $ _____, payable in advance on the _____ day of each month, except when that day falls on a weekend or legal holiday, in which case rent is due on the next business day. Rent shall be paid to _____ at _____, or at such other place as Landlord shall designate from time to time.
   - ❑ a. The form of payment shall be _____.
   - ❑ b. On signing this Agreement, Tenants shall pay to Landlord for the period of _____, 19_____, through _____, 19_____, the sum of $_____ as rent, payable in advance.

6. **Late Charges.** Tenants shall pay Landlord a late charge if Tenants fail to pay the rent in full within _____ days after the date it is due. The late charge shall be $_____, plus $_____ for each additional day that the rent continues to be unpaid. The total late charge for any one month shall not exceed $_____. Landlord does not waive the right to insist on payment of the rent in full on the date it is due.

7. **Returned Check and Other Bank Charges.** In the event any check offered by Tenants to Landlord in payment of rent or any other amount due under this Agreement is returned for lack of sufficient funds, a "stop payment" or any other reason, Tenants shall pay Landlord a returned check charge in the amount of $_____.

8. **Amount and Payment of Deposits.** On signing this Agreement, Tenants shall pay to Landlord the sum of $_____ as a security deposit. Tenants may not, without Landlord's prior written consent, apply this security deposit to the last month's rent or to any other sum due under this Agreement. Within three weeks after Tenants have vacated the premises, Landlord shall furnish Tenants with an itemized written statement of the reasons for, and the dollar amount of, any of the security deposit retained by the Landlord, along with a check for any deposit balance. Under Section 1950.5 of the California Civil Code, Landlord may withhold only that portion of Tenants' security deposit necessary to: (1) remedy any default by Tenants in the payment of rent; (2) repair damages to the premises exclusive of ordinary wear and tear; and (3) clean the premises if necessary.

Landlord shall pay Tenants interest on all security deposits as follows:

❑ a. Under local law, no interest payments are required.

❑ b. Local law requires that interest be paid or credited, which shall occur as follows:

_____

_____

9. Utilities. Tenants shall be responsible for payment of all utility charges, except for the following, which shall be paid by Landlord:

_____

❑ Tenants' gas or electric meter serves area(s) outside of their premises and there are not separate gas and electric meters for Tenants' unit and the area(s) outside their unit. Tenants and Landlord agree as follows:

_____

_____

10. Prohibition of Assignment and Subletting. Tenants shall not sublet any part of the premises or assign this Agreement without the prior written consent of Landlord.

11. Condition of the Premises. Tenants agree to: (1) keep the premises clean and sanitary and in good repair and, upon termination of the tenancy, to return the premises to Landlord in a condition identical to that which existed when Tenants took occupancy, except for ordinary wear and tear; (2) immediately notify Landlord of any defects or dangerous conditions in and about the premises of which they become aware; and (3) reimburse Landlord, on demand by Landlord, for the cost of any repairs to the premises damaged by Tenants or their guests or invitees through misuse or neglect.

Tenants acknowledge that they have examined the premises, including appliances, fixtures, carpets, drapes and paint, and have found them to be in good, safe and clean condition and repair, except as noted here:

_____

_____

_____

_____

12. Possession of the Premises. If, after signing this Agreement, Tenants fail to take possession of the premises, they shall still be responsible for paying rent and complying with all other terms of this Agreement. In the event Landlord is unable to deliver possession of the premises to Tenants for any reason not within Landlord's control, including, but not limited to, failure of prior occupants to vacate or partial or complete destruction of the premises, Tenants shall have the right to terminate this Agreement. In such event, Landlord's liability to Tenants shall be limited to the return of all sums previously paid by Tenants to Landlord.

13. Pets. No animal, bird or other pet shall be kept on the premises without Landlord's prior written consent, except properly trained dogs needed by blind, deaf or physically disabled persons and:

❑ a. None.

❑ b. _____, under the following conditions:

_____

14. Landlord's Access for Inspection and Emergency. Landlord or Landlord's agents may enter the premises in the event of an emergency to make repairs or improvements, supply agreed services and show the premises to prospective buyers or tenants. Except in cases of emergency, Tenants' abandonment of the premises or court order, Landlord shall give Tenants reasonable notice of intent to enter and shall enter only during regular business hours of Monday through Friday from 9:00 a.m. to 6:00 p.m. and Saturday from 10:00 a.m. to 1:00 p.m.

15. **Extended Absences By Tenants.** Tenants agree to notify Landlord in the event that they will be away from the premises for _____ consecutive days or more. During such absence, Landlord may enter the premises at times reasonably necessary to maintain the property and inspect for damage and needed repairs.

16. **Prohibitions Against Violating Laws and Causing Disturbances.** Tenants shall be entitled to quiet enjoyment of the premises. Tenants and their guests or invitees shall not use the premises or adjacent areas in such a way as to: (1) violate any law or ordinance, including laws prohibiting the use, possession or sale of illegal drugs; (2) commit waste or nuisance; or (3) annoy, disturb, inconvenience or interfere with the quiet enjoyment and peace and quiet of any other tenant or nearby resident.

17. **Repairs and Alterations**
    a. Tenants shall not, without Landlord's prior written consent, alter, re-key or install any locks to the premises or install or alter any burglar alarm system. Tenants shall provide Landlord with a key or keys capable of unlocking all such re-keyed or new locks as well as instructions on how to disarm any altered or new burglar alarm system.
    b. Except as provided by law or as authorized by the prior written consent of Landlord, Tenants shall not make any repairs or alterations to the premises.
    ❑ Landlord and Tenants agree to the following:
    _____
    _____
    _____

18. **Damage to the Premises.** In the event the premises are partially or totally damaged or destroyed by fire or other cause, the following shall apply:
    a. If the premises are totally damaged and destroyed, Landlord shall have the option to: (1) repair such damage and restore the premises, with this Agreement continuing in full force and effect, except that Tenants' rent shall be abated while repairs are being made; or (2) give written notice to Tenants terminating this Agreement at any time within thirty (30) days after such damage, and specifying the termination date; in the event that Landlord gives such notice, this Agreement shall expire and all of Tenants' rights pursuant to this Agreement shall cease.
    b. Landlord shall have the option to determine that the premises are only partially damaged by fire or other cause. In that event, Landlord shall attempt to repair such damage and restore the premises within thirty (30) days after such damage. If only part of the premises cannot be used, Tenants must pay rent only for the usable part, to be determined solely by Landlord. If Landlord is unable to complete repairs within thirty (30) days, this Agreement shall expire and all of Tenants' rights pursuant to this Agreement shall terminate at the option of either party.
    c. In the event that Tenants, or their guests or invitees, in any way caused or contributed to the damage of the premises, Landlord shall have the right to terminate this Agreement at any time, and Tenants shall be responsible for all losses, including, but not limited to, damage and repair costs as well as loss of rental income.
    d. Landlord shall not be required to repair or replace any property brought onto the premises by Tenants.

19. **Tenants' Financial Responsibility and Renters' Insurance.** Tenants agree to accept financial responsibility for any loss or damage to personal property belonging to Tenants and their guests and invitees caused by theft, fire or any other cause. Landlord assumes no liability for any such loss. Landlord recommends that Tenants obtain a renter's insurance policy from a recognized insurance firm to cover Tenants' liability, personal property damage and damage to the premises.

20. **Waterbeds.** No waterbed or other item of water-filled furniture shall be kept on the premises without Landlord's written consent.
    ❑ Landlord grants Tenants permission to keep water-filled furniture on the premises. Attachment _____: Agreement Regarding Use of Waterbed is attached to and incorporated into this Agreement by reference.

21. Tenant Rules and Regulations
❑ Tenants acknowledge receipt of, and have read a copy of, tenant rules and regulations, which are labeled Attachment _____ and attached to and incorporated into this Agreement by reference.

22. Payment of Attorney Fees in a Lawsuit. In any action or legal proceeding to enforce any part of this Agreement, the prevailing party ❑ shall not/ ❑ shall recover reasonable attorney fees and court costs.

23. Authority to Receive Legal Papers. Any person managing the premises, the owner and anyone designated by the owner are authorized to accept service of process and receive other notices and demands, which may be delivered to:

❑ a. The manager, at the following address: _____

❑ b. The owner, at the following address: _____

❑ c. The following: _____

24. Additional Provisions

❑ a. None

❑ b. Additional provisions are as follows:
_____
_____
_____

25. Entire Agreement. This document constitutes the entire Agreement between the parties, and no promises or representations, other than those contained here and those implied by law, have been made by Landlord or Tenants. Any modifications to this Agreement must be in writing signed by Landlord and Tenants. The failure of Tenants or their guests or invitees to comply with any term of this Agreement is grounds for termination of the tenancy, with appropriate notice to tenants and procedures as required by law.

_____   _____
Landlord/Manager   Date

_____
Landlord/Manager's Street Address, City, State & Zip

_____   _____
Tenant   Date

_____   _____
Tenant   Date

_____   _____
Tenant   Date

ATTACHMENT _____ TO LEASE OR RENTAL AGREEMENT

Clause _____ .

The following is (choose one):

☐ a continuation of

☐ an addition to

the lease or rental agreement dated _____, 19 _____ :

ATTACHMENT _____ TO LEASE OR RENTAL AGREEMENT

Clause _____.

The following is (choose one):

❑ a continuation of

❑ an addition to

the lease or rental agreement dated _____, 19 _____ :

ATTACHMENT ____: AGREEMENT REGARDING USE OF WATERBED

Landlord and Tenants agree that Tenants may keep water-filled furniture in the premises located at _____
_____ subject to the legal requirements of Civil Code Section 1940.5, key provisions of which are summarized as follows:

1. Insurance

Tenants agree to obtain a valid waterbed insurance policy or certificate of insurance for property damage, with a minimum replacement value of $100,000. Such insurance policy shall be furnished to Landlord prior to installation of the waterbed and shall be maintained in full force and effect until the waterbed is permanently removed from the premises.

2. Weight Limitation

The pressure the waterbed puts on the floor shall not exceed the floor's pounds per square foot weight limitation. The weight shall be distributed on a pedestal or frame which is approximately the same dimensions as the mattress itself.

3. Installation, Moving and Removal

Tenants shall install, maintain and move the waterbed in accordance with the standards of the manufacturer, retailer or state, whichever are most stringent.

4. Notice to and Inspection by Landlord

Tenants agree to give Landlord at least 24 hours written notice of their intention to install, move or remove the waterbed, and shall allow Landlord to be present when this occurs. If anyone other than Tenants installs or moves the waterbed, Tenants shall give Landlord a written installation receipt that states the installer's name, address and any business affiliation.

5. Waterbed Construction Standards

The waterbed shall conform to construction standards imposed by the State Bureau of Home Furnishings and shall display a label to that effect. The waterbed must have been constructed on or after January 1, 1973.

6. Security Deposit

Landlord may increase Tenants' security deposit in an amount equal to an additional one-half month's rent.

_____   _____
Landlord/Manager   Date

_____   _____
Tenant   Date

_____   _____
Tenant   Date

_____   _____
Tenant   Date

LANDLORD/TENANT CHECKLIST—GENERAL CONDITION OF ROOMS

(see reverse side for furnished property)

Street Address _____ Unit Number _____ City _____

	Condition on Arrival	Condition on Departure	Estimated Cost of Repair/Replacement
Living Room			
Floors & Floor Coverings			
Drapes & Window Coverings			
Walls & Ceilings			
Light Fixtures			
Windows, Screens & Doors			
Front Door & Locks			
Smoke Detector			
Fireplace			
Other			
Other			
Kitchen			
Floors & Floor Coverings			
Walls & Ceilings			
Light Fixtures			
Cabinets			
Counters			
Stove/Oven			
Refrigerator			
Dishwasher			
Garbage Disposal			
Sink & Plumbing			
Smoke Detector			
Other			
Other			
Dining Room			
Floors & Floor Covering			
Walls & Ceiling			
Light Fixtures			
Windows, Screens & Doors			
Smoke Detector			
Other			
Other			

	Condition on Arrival		Condition on Arrival	Condition on Departure		Condition on Departure	Estimated Cost of Repair/Replacement
Bathroom(s)	Bath 1		Bath 2	Bath 1		Bath 2	
Floors & Floor Coverings							
Walls & Ceilings							
Windows, Screens & Doors							
Light Fixtures							
Bathtub/Shower							
Sink & Counters							
Toilet							
Other							
Other							
Bedroom(s)	Bedroom 1	Bedroom 2	Bedroom 3	Bedroom 1	Bedroom 2	Bedroom 3	
Floors & Floor Coverings							
Windows, Screens & Doors							
Walls & Ceilings							
Light Fixtures							
Smoke Detectors							
Other							
Other							

	Condition on Arrival	Condition on Departure	Estimated Cost of Repair/Replacement
Other Areas			
Furnace/Heater			
Air Conditioning			
Lawn/Ground Covering			
Garden			
Patio, Terrace, Deck, etc.			
Other			
Other			

❏ Tenants acknowledge that all smoke detectors were tested in their presence and found to be in working order, and that the testing procedure was explained to them. Tenants agree to test all detectors at least once a month and to report any problems to Landlord/Manager in writing. Tenants agree to replace all smoke detector batteries as necessary.

Landlord/Tenant Checklist

LANDLORD/TENANT CHECKLIST—FURNISHINGS

	Condition on Arrival			Condition on Departure			Estimated Cost of Repair/Replacement
Living Room							
Coffee Table							
End Tables							
Lamps							
Chairs							
Sofa							
Other							
Other							
Kitchen							
Broiler pan							
Ice Trays							
Other							
Other							
Dining Area							
Chairs							
Stools							
Table							
Other							
Other							
Bathroom(s)	Bath 1	Bath 2		Bath 1	Bath 2		
Dresser Tables							
Mirrors							
Shower Curtain							
Hamper							
Other							
Other							
Bedroom(s)	Bedroom 1	Bedroom 2	Bedroom 3	Bedroom 1	Bedroom 2	Bedroom 3	
Beds (single)							
Beds (double)							
Chairs							
Chests							
Dressing Tables							
Lamps							
Mirrors							
Night Tables							
Other							
Other							
Other Areas							
Bookcases							
Desks							
Pictures							
Other							
Other							

Use this space to provide any additional explanation: _____

_____

_____

_____

Landlord/Tenant Checklist completed on moving in on _____, 19_____, and approved by:

_____ and _____
Landlord/Manager   Tenant

                                            _____
                                            Tenant

                                            _____
                                            Tenant

Landlord/Tenant Checklist completed on moving out on _____, 19_____, and approved by:

_____ and _____
Landlord/Manager   Tenant

                                            _____
                                            Tenant

                                            _____
                                            Tenant

LANDLORD/TENANT CHECKLIST—GENERAL CONDITION OF ROOMS

(see reverse side for furnished property)

Street Address _____ Unit Number _____ City _____

	Condition on Arrival	Condition on Departure	Estimated Cost of Repair/Replacement
Living Room			
Floors & Floor Coverings			
Drapes & Window Coverings			
Walls & Ceilings			
Light Fixtures			
Windows, Screens & Doors			
Front Door & Locks			
Smoke Detector			
Fireplace			
Other			
Other			
Kitchen			
Floors & Floor Coverings			
Walls & Ceilings			
Light Fixtures			
Cabinets			
Counters			
Stove/Oven			
Refrigerator			
Dishwasher			
Garbage Disposal			
Sink & Plumbing			
Smoke Detector			
Other			
Other			
Dining Room			
Floors & Floor Covering			
Walls & Ceiling			
Light Fixtures			
Windows, Screens & Doors			
Smoke Detector			
Other			
Other			

	Condition on Arrival		Condition on Departure		Estimated Cost of Repair/Replacement
Bathroom(s)	Bath 1	Bath 2	Bath 1	Bath 2	
Floors & Floor Coverings					
Walls & Ceilings					
Windows, Screens & Doors					
Light Fixtures					
Bathtub/Shower					
Sink & Counters					
Toilet					
Other					
Other					

	Condition on Arrival			Condition on Departure			Estimated Cost of Repair/Replacement
Bedroom(s)	Bedroom 1	Bedroom 2	Bedroom 3	Bedroom 1	Bedroom 2	Bedroom 3	
Floors & Floor Coverings							
Windows, Screens & Doors							
Walls & Ceilings							
Light Fixtures							
Smoke Detectors							
Other							
Other							

	Condition on Arrival	Condition on Departure	Estimated Cost of Repair/Replacement
Other Areas			
Furnace/Heater			
Air Conditioning			
Lawn/Ground Covering			
Garden			
Patio, Terrace, Deck, etc.			
Other			
Other			

❑ Tenants acknowledge that all smoke detectors were tested in their presence and found to be in working order, and that the testing procedure was explained to them. Tenants agree to test all detectors at least once a month and to report any problems to Landlord/Manager in writing. Tenants agree to replace all smoke detector batteries as necessary.

LANDLORD/TENANT CHECKLIST—FURNISHINGS

	Condition on Arrival			Condition on Departure			Estimated Cost of Repair/Replacement
Living Room							
Coffee Table							
End Tables							
Lamps							
Chairs							
Sofa							
Other							
Other							
Kitchen							
Broiler pan							
Ice Trays							
Other							
Other							
Dining Area							
Chairs							
Stools							
Table							
Other							
Other							
Bathroom(s)	Bath 1		Bath 2	Bath 1		Bath 2	
Dresser Tables							
Mirrors							
Shower Curtain							
Hamper							
Other							
Other							
Bedroom(s)	Bedroom 1	Bedroom 2	Bedroom 3	Bedroom 1	Bedroom 2	Bedroom 3	
Beds (single)							
Beds (double)							
Chairs							
Chests							
Dressing Tables							
Lamps							
Mirrors							
Night Tables							
Other							
Other							
Other Areas							
Bookcases							
Desks							
Pictures							
Other							
Other							

Use this space to provide any additional explanation: _____
_____
_____
_____

Landlord/Tenant Checklist completed on moving in on _____, 19_____, and approved by:

_____ and _____
         Landlord/Manager   Tenant

                                                 _____
                                                                Tenant

                                                 _____
                                                                Tenant

Landlord/Tenant Checklist completed on moving out on _____, 19_____, and approved by:

_____ and _____
         Landlord/Manager   Tenant

                                                 _____
                                                                Tenant

                                                 _____
                                                                Tenant

DISCLOSURES BY PROPERTY OWNER(S)

The owner(s) of property located at _____
_____
make(s) the following disclosure(s) to prospective tenant(s) and/or employee(s):

❑ **Location near former military base.** State law requires property owners to disclose to all prospective tenants, before they sign any rental agreement or lease, if the property they are seeking to rent is within one mile of a former ordnance area (military base) as defined by California Civil Code Section 1940.7.
Details regarding the former military base near the property listed above are as follows:

_____
_____
_____
_____

❑ **Asbestos.** State law requires property owners who own apartment buildings that have ten or more units and were constructed before 1979 to disclose to all prospective tenants, before they sign any rental agreement or lease, and to all employees who work in the building, if the building contains "asbestos-containing construction materials." The written notice must be given to each employee and tenant individually. (Health & Safety Code Sections 25915-25924.)
Information regarding asbestos in the property listed above is as follows:

_____
_____
_____
_____

_____   _____
Owner's Signature   Date

I have read and received a copy of the above Disclosures By Property Owner(s).

_____   _____
Signature   Date

RECEIPT

Received from _____ :
$ _____ (_____ dollars)
on _____ , 19 _____ .

Received by: _____
                          (signature)

- -

RECEIPT

Received from _____ :
$ _____ (_____ dollars)
on _____ , 19 _____ .

Received by: _____
                          (signature)

- -

RECEIPT

Received from _____ :
$ _____ (_____ dollars)
on _____ , 19 _____ .

Received by: _____
                          (signature)

AMENDMENT TO LEASE OR RENTAL AGREEMENT

This is an Amendment to the lease or rental agreement dated _____, 19_____ (the "Agreement") between _____ ("Landlord") and _____ ("Tenants") regarding property located at _____ ("the premises").

Landlord and Tenants agree to the following changes and/or additions to the Agreement:

In all other respects, the terms of the Agreement shall remain in effect.

_____   _____
Landlord/Manager   Date

_____   _____
Tenant   Date

_____   _____
Tenant   Date

_____   _____
Tenant   Date

AMENDMENT TO LEASE OR RENTAL AGREEMENT

This is an Amendment to the lease or rental agreement dated _____, 19_____ (the "Agreement") between _____ ("Landlord") and _____ ("Tenants") regarding property located at _____ ("the premises").

Landlord and Tenants agree to the following changes and/or additions to the Agreement:

In all other respects, the terms of the Agreement shall remain in effect.

_____   _____
Landlord/Manager   Date

_____   _____
Tenant   Date

_____   _____
Tenant   Date

_____   _____
Tenant   Date

MAINTENANCE/REPAIR REQUEST

Date: _____

Address: _____

Resident's Name: _____

Phone (Home): _____

Phone (Work): _____

Problem: _____

_____

_____

_____

_____

_____

Comments (including best time to make repairs): _____

_____

_____

_____

_____

_____

I authorize entry into my unit to perform the maintenance or repair requested above, in my absence, unless stated otherwise above.

_____
Resident

FOR MANAGEMENT USE

Work done: _____

_____

Time spent: _____ hours

Date completed: _____ , 19 _____

Unable to complete on _____ , 19 _____ because:

_____

_____

_____

_____
Landlord/Manager

MAINTENANCE/REPAIR REQUEST

Date: _____

Address: _____

Resident's Name: _____

Phone (Home): _____

Phone (Work): _____

Problem: _____

_____

_____

_____

_____

_____

Comments (including best time to make repairs): _____

_____

_____

_____

_____

_____

I authorize entry into my unit to perform the maintenance or repair requested above, in my absence, unless stated otherwise above.

_____
Resident

FOR MANAGEMENT USE

Work done: _____

_____

Time spent: _____ hours

Date completed: _____ , 19 _____

Unable to complete on _____ , 19 _____ because:

_____

_____

_____

_____
Landlord/Manager

SECURITY DEPOSIT ITEMIZATION
(Deductions for repairs, cleaning and unpaid rent)
Civil Code Section 1950.5

Date: _____

To: _____   From: _____

_____   _____

_____   _____

Property Address: _____

Rental Period: _____

1. Security Deposit Received: _____ $ _____

2. Interest on deposit (if required by lease or local law): $ _____

3. Total Credit (sum of lines 1 and 2): $ _____

4. Itemized Repairs: _____

   _____
   _____
   _____
   _____
   _____
   _____

   Total Repair Cost: $ _____

5. Necessary Cleaning: _____

   _____
   _____
   _____
   _____
   _____
   _____

   Total Cleaning Cost: $ _____

6. Defaults in rent not covered by any court judgment
   (list dates and rate): _____

   _____
   _____
   _____
   _____
   _____

   Total Rent Defaults: $ _____

7. Amount of Court Judgment for Rent, Costs, Attorney Fees: $ _____

8. Amount Owed (line 3 minus the sum of lines 4, 5, 6 and 7):

   ❏ a. Total Amount Tenant Owes Landlord: $ _____

   ❏ b. Total Amount Landlord Owes Tenant: $ _____

Comments: _____

_____

_____

nolo's SELF-HELP LAW RESOURCES

ESTATE PLANNING & PROBATE

Plan Your Estate With a Living Trust	$19.95	• NEST
Make Your Own Living Trust	$19.95	• LITR
Nolo's Simple Will Book	$17.95	• SWIL
Nolo's Law Form Kits: Wills	$14.95	• KWL
Write Your Will (audio tape)	$14.95	• TWYW
Who Will Handle Your Finances If You Can't?	$19.95	• FINA
How to Probate an Estate (California edition)	$34.95	• PAE
The Conservatorship Book (California edition)	$24.95	• CNSV
5 Ways to Avoid Probate (audio tape)	$14.95	• TPRO

GOING TO COURT

Everybody's Guide to Small Claims Court		
National edition	$16.95	• NSCC
California edition	$16.95	• CSCC
Everybody's Guide to Municipal Court (California edition)	$29.95	• MUNI
Represent Yourself in Court	$29.95	• RYC
Winning in Small Claims Court (audio tape)	$14.95	• TWIN
Fight Your Ticket (California edition)	$18.95	• FYT
Collect Your Court Judgment (California edition)	$19.95	• JUDG
How to Change Your Name (California edition)	$19.95	• NAME
The Criminal Records Book (California edition)	$19.95	• CRIM

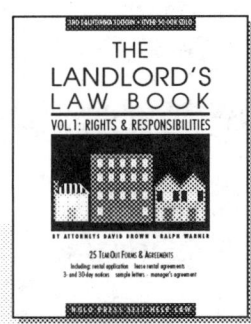

THE LANDLORD'S LAW BOOK: VOL. 1: RIGHTS & RESPONSIBILITIES

California 4th Edition • $32.95 LBRT

The era when a landlord could substitute common sense for a detailed knowledge of the law is gone forever. Everything from the amount you can charge for a security deposit, to terminating a tenancy, to your legal responsibility for the illegal acts of your manager is closely regulated by the law.

This volume covers deposits, leases and rental agreements, inspections (tenant's privacy rights), habitability (rent withholding), ending a tenancy, liability and rent control. Tear-out forms are included.

FAMILY MATTERS

The Living Together Kit	$17.95	• LTK
Divorce & Money	$21.95	• DIMO
A Legal Guide for Lesbian and Gay Couples	$21.95	• LG
Nolo's Pocket Guide to Family Law	$14.95	• FLD
How to Raise or Lower Child Support in California (California edition)	$16.95	• CHLD
How to Adopt Your Stepchild in California (California edition)	$22.95	• ADOP
California Marriage & Divorce Law (California edition)	$19.95	• MARR
The Guardianship Book (California edition)	$19.95	• GB
Divorce: A New Yorker's Guide to Doing It Yourself	$24.95	• NYDIV
How to Do Your Own Divorce		
California edition	$19.95	• CDIV
Texas edition	$17.95	• TDIV

BUSINESS/WORKPLACE

The Legal Guide for Starting & Running a Small Business	$22.95	• RUNS
Sexual Harassment on the Job	$14.95	• HARS
Your Rights in the Workplace	$15.95	• YRW
How to Write a Business Plan	$19.95	• SBS
How to Start Your Own Business: Small Business Law (audio tape)	$14.95	• TBUS
Marketing Without Advertising	$14.00	• MWAD
The Partnership Book	$24.95	• PART
How to Form Your Own Corporation		
California edition	$29.95	• CCOR
New York edition	$24.95	• NYCO
Texas edition	$29.95	• TCOR
The California Nonprofit Corporation Handbook	$29.95	• NON
The California Professional Corporation Handbook	$34.95	• PROF
How to Form A Nonprofit Corporation	$24.95	• NNP
The Independent Paralegal's Handbook	$24.95	• PARA
Getting Started as an Independent Paralegal (two audio tapes)	$44.95	• GSIP

Books with disk

The California Nonprofit Corporation Handbook		
DOS	$39.95	• NPI
MACINTOSH	$39.95	• NPM
How to Form Your Own Florida Corporation		
DOS	$39.95	• FLCO
How to Form Your Own New York Corporation		
DOS	$39.95	• NYCI
MACINTOSH	$69.95	• NYCM
How to Form Your Own Texas Corporation		
DOS	$39.95	• TCI
MACINTOSH	$69.95	• TCM
Software Development: A Legal Guide	$44.95	• SFT

To place an order or receive Nolo's complete catalog, please call: 1-800-992-6656

MONEY MATTERS

Money Troubles: Legal Strategies to Cope With Your Debts	$16.95	MT
How to File for Bankruptcy	$25.95	HFB
Stand Up to the IRS	$21.95	SIRS
Nolo's Law Form Kits: Buy & Sell Contracts	$9.95	KCONT
Nolo's Law Form Kits: Loan Agreements	$14.95	KLOAN
Nolo's Law Form Kits: Personal Bankruptcy	$14.95	KBNK
Nolo's Law Form Kits: Power of Attorney	$14.95	KPA
Nolo's Law Form Kits: Rebuild Your Credit	$14.95	KCRD
Simple Contracts for Personal Use	$16.95	CONT

OLDER AMERICANS

Beat the Nursing Home Trap	$18.95	ELD
Social Security, Medicare & Pensions	$15.95	SOA

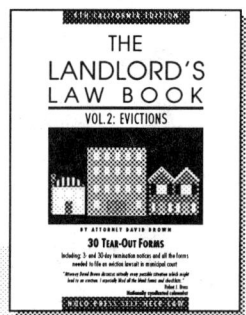

THE LANDLORD'S LAW BOOK, VOL. 2 EVICTIONS

California 4th edition • $32.95 • LBEV

This book shows you step-by-step how to go to court and evict a tenant. It explains all the legal grounds for eviction and has a special section on rent control laws. Includes all the tear-out forms and instructions you need to prepare and serve the tenant with a proper legal notice, file an eviction lawsuit, handle a contested case and collect the money judgment.

THE NEIGHBORHOOD

Neighbor Law: Fences, Trees, Boundaries & Noise	$14.95	NEI
Dog Law	$12.95	DOG
Safe Homes, Safe Neighborhoods: Stopping Crime Where You Live	$14.95	SAFE

LANDLORDS & TENANTS

Tenants' Rights (California edition)	$15.95	CTEN
The Landlord's Law Book, Vol. 1: Rights & Responsibilities (California edition)	$32.95	LBRT
The Landlord's Law Book, Vol. 2: Evictions (California edition)	$32.95	LBEV
Nolo's Law Form Kit: Leases & Rental Agreements (California edition)	$14.95	KLEAS

HOMEOWNERS

How To Buy a House in California (California edition)	$19.95	BHCA
For Sale By Owner (California edition)	$24.95	FSBO
The Deeds Book (California edition)	$15.95	DEED
Homestead Your House (California edition)	$9.95	HOME

PATENT, COPYRIGHT & TRADEMARK

Trademark: How to Name A Business & Product	$29.95	TRD
Patent It Yourself	$36.95	PAT
The Inventor's Notebook	$19.95	INOT
The Copyright Handbook	$24.95	COHA

IMMIGRATION

How to Get a Green Card: Legal Ways to Stay in the U.S.A.	$19.95	GRN

JUST FOR FUN

29 Reasons Not to Go to Law School	$9.95	29R
Poetic Justice: The Funniest, Meanest Things Ever Said About Lawyers	$8.95	PJ
Devil's Advocates: The Unnatural History of Lawyers	$12.95	DA

CONSUMER

Nolo's Pocket Guide to Consumer Rights (California edition)	$12.95	CAG
Nolo's Pocket Guide to California Law	$10.95	CLAW
How to Win Your Personal Injury Claim	$24.95	PICL
Nolo's Law Form Kit: Hiring Child Care & Household Help	$14.95	KCHLD

RESEARCH/REFERENCE

Legal Research: How To Find and Understand the Law	$19.95	LRES
Legal Research Made Easy (2½ hr. videotape & 40-page manual)	$89.95	LRME
Legal Breakdown: 40 Ways to Fix Our Legal System	$8.95	LEG

SOFTWARE

WillMaker		
DOS	$69.95	WI5
MACINTOSH	$69.95	WM5
Windows	$69.95	WIW5
Nolo's Living Trust (MACINTOSH)	$79.95	LTM1
Nolo's Personal RecordKeeper		
DOS	$49.95	FRI3
MACINTOSH	$49.95	FRM3
Nolo's Partnership Maker		
DOS	$129.95	PAGI1
California Incorporator		
DOS	$129.00	INCI

FAX: 1-800-645-0895   **General information: 1-510-549-1976**

GET 25% OFF YOUR NEXT PURCHASE

RECYCLE YOUR OUT-OF-DATE LAW FORM KIT

It's important to have the most current legal information. Because laws and legal procedures change often, we update our law form kits regularly. To help keep you up-to-date we are extending this special offer. Cut out and mail the title portion of the cover of any old Nolo law form kit with your next order and we'll give you a 25% discount off the retail price of ANY new Nolo law form kit or book you purchase directly from us. For current prices and editions call us at 1-800-992-6656.

This offer is to individuals only.

ORDER FORM

Name

Address (UPS to street address, Priority Mail to P.O. boxes)

Catalog Code	Quantity	Item	Unit price	Total

Subtotal		
Local Sales tax (California residents only)		
Shipping & handling		
2nd day UPS		
TOTAL		

PRICES SUBJECT TO CHANGE

KLEAS

FOR FASTER SERVICE, USE YOUR CREDIT CARD AND OUR TOLL-FREE NUMBERS:

Monday-Friday, 7 a.m. to 6 p.m. Pacific Time
Order line   1 (800) 992-6656
General Information   1 (510) 549-1976
Fax us your order   1 (800) 645-0895

SHIPPING & HANDLING
$4.00   1 item
$5.00   2-3 items
+$.50   each additional item
Allow 2-3 weeks for delivery

IN A HURRY?
UPS 2nd day delivery is available:
Add $5.00 (contiguous states) or $8.00 (Alaska & Hawaii) to your regular shipping and handling charges

METHOD OF PAYMENT
☐ Check enclosed
☐ VISA ☐ Mastercard ☐ Discover Card ☐ American Express

Account Number   Expiration Date

Signature Authorizing

Phone

NOLO PRESS / 950 PARKER STREET / BERKELEY CA 94710

ABOUT NOLO PRESS

The leading publisher of self-help law books and software since 1971

Nolo Press exists because two former Legal Aid lawyers, fed up with the public's lack of affordable legal information and advice, began writing understandable, easy-to-use, self-help law books more than 20 years ago. Now, Nolo publishes books, form kits, software and audio and videotapes. But the purpose has never changed: to take the mystery out of law and make it available to everyone.

About 60 of us work in a converted clock factory in Berkeley, California. We regularly tackle new self-help law products and, because laws change constantly, work to keep our backlist (80 titles) up to date. We encourage our customers to suggest ideas for improvement, which we can incorporate into new editions.

Lawyers sometimes compare self-help law to do-it-yourself brain surgery. Nonsense—it's much more akin to choosing an over-the-counter remedy for a routine illness. Whether they want to relieve a headache, prepare their income tax returns, build a room on a house or handle their own bankruptcy case, people can do much of the work themselves if they have good, reliable information.

Twenty years' experience has only strengthened our belief that law, like any other body of information, can be broken down and organized into small, easily-digested bits. Once that's done, it's relatively easy to find answers to legal questions, whether they concern a divorce, trademark or dog bite dispute.

Nolo's mission is far from a radical idea. Every American's right to know the law—without paying a lawyer—is a cornerstone of our democracy. Making the process easier is what we are here for.